Fortis Momentum

A Spiritually Inspirational Self-Help Book of Prayers, Meditations, Thoughts, and Strategies for Christianity

ISBN: 1466414081
ISBN-13: 9781466414082
Library of Congress Control Number: 2014906805
CreateSpace Independent Publishing Platform
North Charleston, South Carolina

Fortis Momentum

Chris Downs

This book is dedicated to you.
For others…for God.

Directions (Table of Contents):

Introduction

For those who don't know how to pray, or those who would like to know how to pray better; for those who have questions about the Bible or life in general; for those who want to keep it simple, and for those who want to delve deeper into God's Word. For those who want to stand strong as a Christian and for those looking for something that's different from your usual Christian book, this was written for you! It isn't your typical book…it's actually a series of sections designed on the acronym "KISS," or "Keep It Simple, Stupid" while listing a vast array of biblical verses for the reader who seeks to go even further into God's Word and grow a much stronger relationship with Him…I strongly encourage you to read them as you have time.

It's a journey to take inside your mind, a set of stepping-stones and a compass designed to provide you with tools for the true journey…your life! It's as simple as you want it to be, and can go as complex as you might want it to. However you use this book, customize it to your own unique life. When it has a prayer, customize it to fit what you're going through. When there's a thought of something to ponder, always keep God in mind and let your headaches go away as you find God's peace in the prayers listed next to each thought. When you want to be prepared, use the tools this book has to offer, and you'll be better equipped for the journey you have ahead of you…the great life that God has called you to! And best of all, this book isn't just for you…it's for all those you'll encounter on the rest of your journey through this life!

Add to this book prayers of your own, other verses that come to mind, ideas or thoughts you think of that you'll want to remember, and know that when something isn't elaborated enough, it's because I want you to find the meaning from within your own heart, so that it applies directly to your own unique, personal life.

"Have I not commanded you? Be strong and courageous. Do not be afraid; do not be discouraged, for the Lord your God will be with you wherever you go."

– Joshua 1:9 NIV

START:

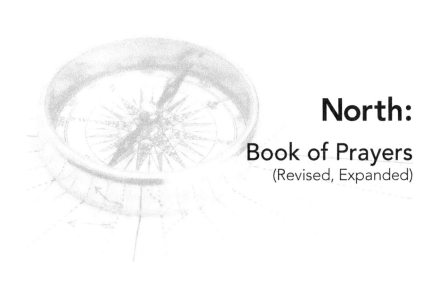

North:
Book of Prayers
(Revised, Expanded)

Let's open up in prayer:

Dear Father, who is in Heaven, thank you for
this glorious day. Thank you that we are alive
and that you are dwelling within us. There is
no one greater than you, so please help us as
we set out on this journey to become even better
at praying. Help us to see things the way you
view, hear things the way you hear, and most
importantly, to do things in accordance with
your will and in your will, alone.
Amen.

(The rest of the book will follow this pattern,
that is, immediately starting with prayer.
It is, after all, a Book of Prayers).

Note:
For those who wish to delve deeper,
Have a Bible or BibleGateway.com ready
And study the scriptures mentioned.

Contents:

Part I
What is Prayer?

Dear Lord,

Please help the rest of this day to go well. Please help me to understand what the author is trying to say, but only in your view. Please help me to use the help of this book to enhance my prayer life, and to ultimately draw closer to you. Please have everything that's done be in accordance with your will and yours alone because your will is perfect. Thank you for loving me, Lord.

We all know what prayer is, right? Wrong. When we usually think of prayer, all that comes to mind is "Dear Lord, problem, need, etc. Amen." When in truth, praying can be so many different things. In the Bible, prayer is seen as a calling on God, a time for confession, a time for requesting, time for the Holy Spirit to pray on our behalf, thanksgiving for food, a time to remember Jesus before taking communion, a time for pleading to God, a time for complaining (but also know that the prayers of the wicked are not heard by God). Prayer is responding to God for events that shape our lives, as there was first life before we first prayed, and then we gained something to pray about, and began to petition the Lord. God invites us to pray. In fact, it's one of the basic gifts we have...the ability to speak with God. Prayer, as a form of communicating with God, is also, then, a time for listening for God. There are the times when we don't know what to pray, so we let the Spirit pray on our behalf, as when we can't find the words to tell God, but we know our hearts are crying out to Him. Prayer can be in thanks for receiving gifts from God and prayer can also be thanking God for going through trials and tribulations; knowing that what you just went through has strengthened your faith.

Our Lord and Savior Jesus Christ gave plenty of examples of prayer; when he was in the desert 40 days and nights, when he was being tested, when he went through the passion (crucifixion), and throughout his daily life we can rest assured that Jesus prayed to the Father at many various times.

You can pray to give thanks, pray to ask for something, pray by fasting or pray by simply crying out to God. When it comes to prayer, there's really no limit to what you can do, that is, as long as your prayers are in alignment with God's will (as in, not wicked and deceitful and of the enemy).

Abraham prayed for a child, Samson prayed for strength. Joshua prayed that the sun would stand still. Moses prayed for his enemies to be scattered. When it comes to prayer, there's really no limit on what we can pray, as long as it's in accordance with God's will (and with good intentions).

Part II
Leading

Dear Lord,

Please guide, direct, surround and protect us completely with legions upon infinite legions of your mighty guardian angels. With your love, your heart, your joy, peace, patience, wisdom, knowledge, understanding and discernment. With your powerful Holy Spirit, and all the gifts, ministries, powers and abilities of it. Keep us on the straight path towards your Holy Kingdom and help us that we might come to glorify your name, which is the name above all names.

GUIDE

Please *guide* us, so that we know the right paths. Guide us to know which way is right and shed light on which ways are evil. Guide us so strongly that there is no confusion in our hearts as to what you would have us do.

Where to look: Psalm 23:3, 25:5,9; Isaiah 42:16; John 16:13

DIRECT

Please *direct* us so that our human nature doesn't overpower us and steer us into the wrong direction. Direct us as a composer directs his music. Make our hearts sing praises to your name even when the path you have us on may seem like hell itself is caving in over us. Direct us towards a better understanding of who you are, in us, and who we are to be in you and your Kingdom.

Where to Look: Proverbs 4:25, 20:24; Isaiah 48:17; Jeremiah 10:23; 2 Thessalonians 3:5

SURROUND

Please *surround* us so that first and foremost, it is you we see in our lives wherever we look. Make yourself known to us, even in the darkest of time. Surround us with so much of who you are, and surround us with what you are. You are the calm in the eye of the storm. You are the breath reached for from the depths of the sea. Your Holiness in itself is perfection, so please surround us with your Holy Spirit. Have it dwell deep within our hearts, in our innermost parts to where it will flood out to all those around us. Surround us completely, leaving no opening for evil. Then have us surround the globe to do your will.

Where to Look: Psalm 5:12, 32:7, 10; 89:8, 125:2

PROTECT

Please, Heavenly Father, *protect* us from the enemy. For you are our salvation, your Spirit, is our comforter, and your armor, our protection. As we have just asked you to surround us, now please protect us. Protect our hearts from the pains of life. Protect our minds from sinister and immoral thoughts. Protect our eyes from seeing what is meant to be unseen, and protect our ears from hearing that which is of the world. Please protect us on all fronts, so that we might rest assured in knowing that it is the creator of all who is protecting us; that we might come to praise your name for this very protection and the love you give.

Where to Look: Deuteronomy 23:14; Job 5:21; Psalm 5:11;
12:5, 7; 32:7; 40:11; 41:2; 69:29; 91:14; Proverbs 2:11;
John 17:11; 17 15; 2 Thessalonians 3:3

Afterward

We need God to guide, direct, surround and protect us at all times. There's never one second in life when we don't need this. In fact, it's when we say we don't need this that we let our guard down and the devil goes to haphazardly attack us on all fronts. To conclude this segment of the book, I encourage you to ask God to guide, direct, surround and protect you daily. Pray for this as soon as you wake up. Put on your full armor so that you will be prepared for any spiritual attack the enemy will give you, and prepare for battle. Spiritual battle, that is.

Part III
Healing

Dear Savior,

Please be with us as we open up in prayer. Please forgive us of our past sins and help us to continually be purified through the fire of your Holy Spirit. Have us be continually molded more to the forms that you have intended for us. In this current moment, we need healing that is unseen. Physically, our bodies always need healing. Mentally, our minds could always use some rest. Emotionally, it's better to be high on the Holy Spirit than high in anger. And spiritually, so we can proclaim having a clean bill of health over our spirits. Heal us in every way possible so that we can better serve you.

Where to Look: Jeremiah 33:6

PHYSICALLY

Please, Lord of Lords, heal us *physically* so that we can be capable of doing your will in this world. Heal our bodies and renew them with strength to go on and continue working for you, serving you and your kingdom and helping those around us. Give us the energy we need in abundance so that we might be able to share it with others.

Where to Look: Matthew 4:23; 9:35; Luke 6:19

MENTALLY

Please, Name Above All Names, heal us *mentally* so that we reason in sound mind, not in conformation to this world's train of thought, but considering only your will and wisdom.

Where to Look: Luke 6:19; 9:6; 13:32

EMOTIONALLY

Please, Jesus, hear our calls. We need you to heal us *emotionally*. The world has cursed against us and it seems to never give up. It is a constant burden hearing all the negatives of life that hinder us from growing closer to you. We need you to heal us emotionally so that we can remain thankful and joyously grateful for you and what you do. We need you to heal us emotionally so that we can only feel what you would have us feel, so our hearts can become better in-sync with yours. We love you, so please help us to love you more.

Where to Look: John 5:1; 6:2; 7:23; 9:13

SPIRITUALLY

Please, Holy One, heal us *spiritually* so that we might stay strong *with you* to stay strong *for you*. Please heal us spiritually so that even more of your great and powerful Holy Spirit can dwell within us. Heal us spiritually so much that no dim light shines, but only the brightest possible light so that when we do shine, those who are at a greater distance can still see your amazing work in us. Keep us growing spiritually to help us avoid growing in sin. Keep us in high hopes, knowing that it is you we serve, so that our faith may remain strong and expectant to the rewards you have in store for us, even though we may not understand you and your ever-so-specific timing with which the world turns.

Where to Look: 1 Corinthians 12:9, 28

Afterward

We all need God to heal us physically, mentally, spiritually and emotionally at different times in our lives. We also need different kinds of healing, but since we are supposed to pray for others, I find it easier to just include them all in my daily prayers. This is why I pray with "we", and "us", instead of "I" most of the time. I find it's easier to pray for the group as a whole, when praying for generalities such as healing. That's not to say that someone struggling with an illness doesn't deserve their own unique prayer, because they do.

Part IV
Readiness

Dear Christ, King of Kings,
Forgive us, use us, minister to us and through us, and thank you.

Where to Look: Psalm 130:4

FORGIVENESS

Please *forgive* us of all our sins: past, present and future. Renew our minds so that we think only thoughts that you would approve of. Forgive our wrongs against others, but most importantly help us to understand that any time we sin, it is not others we are hurting as much as it is you we hurt. Please forgive us for being unable to grasp your will at times, and please forgive us our impatience with your timing. Please forgive us any sins we might have committed, and have currently forgotten. Help us to be forgiving, as you are forgiving of us. And most importantly, help us to always remember *why* we're forgiven...because you died and rose from the cross.

Where to Look: Matthew 26:28; Luke 1:77; Acts 13:38; 26:18; Ephesians 1:7; Colossians 1:14; Hebrews 9:22

USE US

Please *use* us. Use us to do your will and to fulfill your will in this world. There are not enough servants in your Kingdom, so please help us to become better at recruiting new helpers. It's always better to have a new Christian's helping hands join ours in service.

Please help us to always gladly accept being used by you and to always remain joyful in that it is YOU who uses us.

Where to Look: Proverbs 10:7; Mark 4:24; Luke 6:38; 2 Corinthians 2:14; 1 Peter 4:10

MINISTER

Please *minister* to us daily, so that we might minister to those around us. In your using of us, have us minister when the time is right. Show us who to minister to and how to minister. Teach us what only you can teach, and give us what we need to do your will. Help us to bring others out from the darkness of this world and into the light, which is the truth of who you are. The truth of who you are is in the Gospel, so please help us gain more insight and discernment about it as we read and study your Word. Please give us the courage and audacity to minister with energy and to always be gladly accepting of anyone whom you have sent to minister to us. Also, keep our ears closed to false prophets, as they are omnipresent in this world. Instead, help us to minister to them, that they might become Christians someday.

Where to Look: Deuteronomy 18:5, 7; Isaiah 56:6; 61:6; Jeremiah 33:22; Romans 15:14, 16; 2 Corinthians 3:6; 1 Timothy 4:6

THANKS

Thank you for who you are. Thank you for what you do. Thank you for giving us the first life, and dying on the cross to secure our next life. Thank you for unconditionally loving us. Thank you for always being there for us. Thank you that we are able to worship you, and thank you for seeing our worship of you as acceptable. None of us deserve you or any piece of you, so

THANK YOU for being the way you are with us...even when we don't understand you.

Where to Look: 1 Chronicles 16:34; 29:13; Psalm 7:17; 9:1; 69:30; 95:2; 100:4; 106:1; 107:8; 118:21; Jeremiah 30:19; Romans 6:7; 1 Corinthians 10:16; 15:57; 2 Corinthians 2:14; 4:15; 9:11, 15; Philemon 1:4; Revelation 4:9; 7:12; 11:17; 1 Thessalonians 5:18; Ephesians 5:20; Philippians 4:6; Colossians 1:2

Afterward

We all know we need forgiveness, so it's always important to pray for this in every walk of life. Not just for us, but for the forgiveness of others as well. Also know that the only unforgiveable sins are taking the mark of the beast (Revelation 14:9-12) and blaspheming the Holy Spirit (Mark 3:29). When it comes to asking God to use us, this can be one highly dangerous prayer. Expect attacks from the devil when you pray this one, but know that if you're being used to do God's work, you're in His will. If you're in His will, He'll protect you. So don't fear the devil. We should always minister at every chance we get, and also praise the Lord every time we spot a blessing.

Part V

Lord's Prayer

"Our Father,
in heaven, hallowed be your name, your kingdom come, your will be done, on earth as it is in heaven. Give us today our daily bread. And forgive us our debts, as we also have forgiven our debtors. And lead us not into temptation, but deliver us from the evil one." (Matthew 6:9-13 NIV)

IN HEAVEN

OUR Father, you are in *Heaven*. Above all creation, looking down at us and unconditionally loving us, You are higher than the highest king, and everything is below you. In your kingdom lies the truth for how things one day on this earth will be.

YOUR WILL

Your will be done. On this earth, and in my heart.

THIS DAY

Give us this day (life), all that we need. All the food, all the shelter, all the love and comfort. Wisdom and insight. All the energy, all the blessings, all the light to see, and all the needs we have. However, do not give too much that we may feel as though we have no need for you, and also, not too little that we might come to curse your name. But please give us exactly what we need so that we aren't deprived or spoiled, but instead blessed with all we need to do your will in this life.

FORGIVE US

Father, *forgive* us as we forgive others. Help us to be forgiving, no matter how difficult it may seem, but only forgive us when we truly deserve. That is, when we have done every-thing in our power to no longer commit the sin that drives you away from us. Please make us humble and contrite. You never leave or forsake us, but we must always keep on cleans-ing ourselves to be even better for you, that we might have more of you to dwell in us.

TEMPTATION

Lead us not into *temptation*. Temptation to commit sin. Temptation to hurt others in any way. Temptation to curse or cuss. Temptation to sway from walking on the righteous path. Temptation to ignore you. Temptation to forget what you've promised us. Temptation to shun your Word. Temptation to listen to the enemy's lies. Temptation to over indulge in some-thing. Temptation to harm our bodies in any way. Temptation to be lazy when that free time could be used to glorify your name. Temptation to eat too much. Temptation to do anything which would in any way hinder our growth in you, through you, by you, for you.

DELIVER

Deliver us from the evil one–Satan, Lucifer, el Diablo, etc.

Afterward

Almost everyone knows the Lord's Prayer. What they don't know is how to make good use of it. Break it down and apply it to your life. Apply it to what situations you currently are facing and I promise you, God will respond. This is not just prayer for yourself and for others…it's intercessory prayer for the world.

Part VI
Global

Abba, Father, Jesus, Lord,

Help us to pray for the whole world.

Help us to pray for those in need.

Help us to pray for those who can't pray.

Help us to pray for those who won't pray.

Help us to pray what you, yourself pray.

Help us to pray, continually, from day to day.

Where to Look: Matthew 5:3-11; Luke 6:20-22, 28; John 13:17; 20:29; Acts 20:35; 1 Peter 39; 14; Revelation 1:3; Psalm 5:2; 72:17; 84:12; 128:2; 132:15; Proverbs 14:21; 22:9; Deuteronomy 24:19; 1:11; 7:13; 14:29; 15:4, 10, 14; 1 Chronicles 4:10; 17:27; 2 Chronicles 31:10

BLESS

Dear Lord, thank you for food, shelter and water. Please give food, shelter and water to all those millions around the world who are without any of these right now. Please remove from their lives the obstacles, which keep them from having food, shelter, and water. All those in the 3rd world and beyond. All those who are unseen by us, but seen by you. Those who have been neglected in this life. Bless them that they might praise your name on high. Bless them with an overabundance of your love. Bless them.

Where to Look: Genesis 28:3-1, 14; Exodus 23:25; Numbers 6:24

POUR OUT

Father, please pour out all your many blessings in, on, and around everyone to the point that your blessings flood out onto those around them. Pour out your Holy Spirit on this corrupt, vile world so much that people would jump in the streets praising your name. Pour out your love on this world, that it might know true love.

Where to Look: Isaiah 44:3; Proverbs 1:23; Ezekiel 39:29; Joel 2:28-29; Zechariah 12:10; Malachi 3:10; Acts 2:17-18, 33; 10:45; Romans 5:5; 1 Timothy 1:14

GRACE

Lord, God, please pour out your grace on this world that it would recognize you. You open your hands freely to those who run to you, but I am asking you to tempt them so strongly so they will run to you. Give them just enough of your grace, and in such a way that when they spot it, they can't help but acknowledge that it is grace from you. Of you, by you, through you, and ultimately: for you.

Where to Look: Psalm 45:2; Zechariah 12:10; John 1:16-17; Acts; 4:33; 6:8; 11:23; 14:3; 15:11; 20:24; Romans 1:5; 3:24; 5:2, 15, 17, 20, 21; 6:14-15; 1 Corinthians 16:23; 2 Corinthians 4:5; 8:7; 1 Timothy 1:12; Ephesians 1:7; 2:5, 7, 8; 4:7; 2 Thessalonians 2:16; Titus 2:11; 3:7; Hebrews 4:16; 10:29; 12:15; James 4:6; 1 Peter 4:19; 2 Peter 3:18

RENEWING

Please Messiah, Savior, Redeemer, spread a new mindset throughout this world. Help all the earth's inhabitants experience a renewing of their minds. Renew them in such a way that they begin to see you in their everyday walks of life. Renew their energy to that of a child's, to the point where procrastination no longer has a place in their minds. Renew them to get rid of their old ways of thinking, that all their new thoughts would be completely and totally thoughts, which only you, the perfect one, would approve of. Renew them.

Where to Look: Romans 12:2

UNDERSTANDING

Please Lord, give us all in this world a true understanding of who you are. No matter how you do it, just do it. Help us to see you in all your many forms, and to see you where you are invisible, but clearly at work. Help us to see and understand your will in this life and to constantly be preparing for the next.

Where to Look: Exodus 31:3; 1 Chronicles 22:12; Psalm 111:10; 119:34, 73, 104, 144, 169; 147:5; Proverbs 2:6, 11; 3:5, 13, 21; 4:1, 5, 7; 9:10; Isaiah 11:2; Mark 12:33; Philemon 1:6; 1 Corinthians 14:15; Ephesians 1:8; 1 John 5:20; Colossians 1:9; 2:2

Afterward

There are people in countries where being a Christian can get you sent out to be executed. So first of all, I prefer to be thankful that I'm in a country where I can worship God freely. Second of all, I choose to use this freedom to spend time praying for those who can't pray for themselves. You don't have to do this, but know we all need the prayer of others sometime or another, so please, at least try this out for change.

Part VII

What to Pray When...

What to Pray When:

When we are afraid:

Recite Psalm 34:4 "I sought the Lord, and he answered me; he delivered me from all my fears." (NIV) Then pray: "Lord, please remove any fears that I'm feeling. Bring me to trust in you more. I know my flesh has me afraid that _____ is going to happen, but I know that in all things, you work for the good of those who love you. Help me to no longer be afraid knowing that you, *you who created the Heavens and the earth* are watching over me. Any fear I have is from the devil. Fear is doubting that you will protect me, so please help me to only fear you and what you would let happen to me if I go against your will. I have no reason to fear anything other than you because you are above all."

When we are feeling anxious:

Recite Philippians 4:6 "Do not be anxious about anything, but in every situation, by prayer and petition, with thanksgiving, present your requests to God." (NIV) And then pray: "Dear Lord, please rid me of any and all anxiety. I have no need to be anxious, though it feels almost impossible to get rid of. I know that you are above all, and that things will work out in *your* will and in *your* timing; ultimately for *your* glory, so I have no reason to worry. The battle is already won through the cross, so please give me the peace to know that in your timing, things are going to turn out for the best.

When we fear falling back into sin:

Recite 1 John 1:8-9 "If we claim to be without sin, we deceive ourselves and the truth is not in us. If we confess our sins, he is faithful and just and will forgive us our sins and purify us from all unrighteousness." (NIV) Then pray: "Father, please forgive me for my sins. I know not all the wrong I've done against you, but I am truly sorry for what you have shown me to be wrong acts on my part. Please help rid me of the initial seeding desire to commit sin, so that it might be easier for me to not sin anymore. It is impossible for me to be made perfect in this life, but through your grace I know I can be purified. Please strengthen me in the way I need in order to refrain from sinning again, and if at all possible, remove any and all temptation the enemy has for me to try and trick me to commit new sins. Thank you Lord for understanding, I love you. Please help me to love you more."

When we sin:

Recite Psalm 51:1-2 "Have mercy on me, O God, according to your unfailing love; according to your great compassion blot out my transgressions. For I have sinned. Wash away all my iniquity and cleanse me from my sin." (NIV) Then pray: "Dear Lord, you are perfect; I am not. I am weak and need you to strengthen me. I need you to help me grow stronger so that the next time the temptation to sin arises, I will be strong enough to defeat it. I need more of you in my life, as the more of you I have, the stronger I become. I pray right now to surrender to you, asking you to enter my heart again and cleanse me from all my sins. Please guard my heart from the evil desires of this world and help me to be pure in your sight."

When we need to rid our lives of those "evil spirits":

Recite Luke 10:20 "However, do not rejoice that the spirits submit to you, but rejoice that your names are written in heaven." (NIV). And know that the word "spirits," does not necessarily refer to demons, but think of them as how there are the spirits of anger, hatred, vengeance, etc., and know whether or not evil spirits are in your life, or in the lives of those who you deal with, please pray: "I rebuke all evil from my life, all those spirits of evil and their ways that the enemy has woven into my existence. I rebuke them and command them to scatter and to flee and to return to the pit of hell from which they came from and to never return to my life again, in the name and power, by the blood, stripes and authority of the Lord God, Jesus Christ and the Holy Spirit. It is done; amen."

When we feel depressed:

Recite Psalm 43:5 "Why, my soul, are you downcast? Why so disturbed within me? Put your hope in God, for I will yet praise him, my Savior and my God." (NIV) Then pray: "My Savior and my God, please help me to feel the comfort only your Spirit can give. Please bless me with your love, compassion, and cares. I seek you and you are all I need to be happy."

When we feel homesick or alone and afraid:

Recite Hebrews 13:5 "...Never will I leave you; never will I forsake you." (NIV) And then pray: "Thanks be to God, who is always at my side. Lord, you carry me when I'm too weak to even walk. You provide food when I'm all alone. You truly are all I need and I'm asking you to provide a way out from this sorrow and pain I'm feeling. Please give me something to fill the void, something of you, a fellow Christian friend, or just a random passerby to comfort me in this time of loneliness and uncertainty. I know that you will provide, but when you do, please make it known so I can praise you."

When we need peace and comfort:

Recite John 16:33 "I have told you these things, so that in me you may have peace. In this world you will have trouble. But take heart! I have overcome the world." (NIV) Then pray: "Lord God, I need the peace and comfort that only you can give. I need it in the very core of who I am. Life feels like it's a constant battle right now and I can't seem to find any peace. I have too much on my schedule and I know I should give more of that time to you. Please at least give me rest on the Sabbath. For I know not how to make peace for myself; only you can give true comfort. Please surround me with your glorious Holy Spirit and let me feel it dwelling within my innermost parts."

When we need guidance:

Recite Isaiah 30:21 "Whether you turn to the right or to the left, your ears will hear a voice behind you, saying, 'This is the way; walk in it.'" (NIV) And pray: "Dear Lord, please guide me so that I know I'm heading in the right direction. Please make it abundantly clear what it is that you have planned for me to do here; please show me my purpose. I'd prefer if you took control of my life 'cause right now I simply don't feel like I'm able to guide it myself. Please pull me in the right direction and if it's in your will, send a helper to aid me. However, keep me from the enemy's traps so I don't fall."

When we have doubt in God:

Recite Hebrews 11:1 "Now faith is confidence in what we hope for and assurance about what we do not see." (NIV) Then pray: "Father, I'm sorry for doubting you. I pray and ask that you would help grow my faith, for it is too small right now. The world has led me to start doubting you and I know this is the work of the enemy, so please, do what it takes to make me believe in you with faith like a child. Help me to grow so strong that nothing could ever again make me question why it's you I choose to worship. You have chosen me to worship you, that's my purpose, to glorify your name, so please make me worthy of doing that task."

When we need to keep on keepin' on:

Recite Mark 13:13 "Everyone will hate you because of me, but the one who stands firm to the end will be saved." (NIV) Then pray: "Lord God, I feel like giving up. I've come so far, and am almost done with what I set out to do, but I don't feel like it's worth it anymore. I need you to renew my spirit, to make my spirit steadfast in your will. I need to be reassured of why I'm doing what I'm doing and you are the best one to show me. So I ask humbly for you to grab ahold of my life and take control; push me past the finish line and keep the gold medal in my sight so I never lose track of why I'm doing what I'm doing."

When we bring bad stuff into our homes:

Recite Hebrews 6:8 "But land that produces thorns and thistles is worthless and is in danger of being cursed. In the end it will be burned." (NIV) and pray: "God please help me to make my house holy. Please help me to cleanse it of (pornography, drugs, alcohol if it's a problem, or whatever it is that I have in it, that I should not; whatever it is that causes me to sin or is a sin). Please help me to keep my house clean so that my walk, and the walk of those who enter my house may not be jeopardized by explicit sinful material.

When we feel like taking vengeance:

Recite Romans 12:17-19 "Do not repay anyone evil for evil. Be careful to do what is right in the eyes of everyone. If it is possible, as far as it depends on you, live at peace with everyone. Do not take revenge, my dear friends, but leave room for God's wrath, for it is written: 'It is mine to avenge, I will repay,' says the Lord." (NIV) Then pray: "Father, I am sorry for thinking it's my right to avenge anything. I know that I can hurt someone physically or verbally, and it would do damage, but I know that would only cause more sin. I know that you are just in your judgments, so I put this situation into your hands, knowing that things will work out better for me this way. I put my actions into your hands so that a little anger and bitterness won't get in the way of me growing my faith. I pray that those whom I want revenge on will come to know you."

When we want to worship more and/or or better:

Recite John 4:23 "Yet a time is coming and has now come when the true worshipers will worship the Father in spirit and truth, for they are the kind of worshippers the Father seeks." (NIV) and then pray: "Dear Lord, please fill us with your joy. Please give us so much joy in abundance that we won't be able to contain our praises for you. Have us praise you day and night for all the great blessings you bestow upon us, and help us to always keep in mind a countenance of all our blessings. Surely as the sun rises each day, so you have blessed us daily."

When we fear being tempted:

Recite Matthew 26:41 "Watch and pray so that you will not fall into temptation. The spirit is willing, but the flesh is weak." (NIV), and pray: "Dear Lord, thank you for keeping me from temptation so far, but I fear I might give into my fleshly desires and fall for temptation very soon. I know the spirit is much stronger, so I'm asking you to renew a steadfast spirit within me and deliver me out from the evil desires of this world. I pray and ask that you would watch over my every step, to make sure that I keep my eyes focused on what matters, which is salvation, and living a holy and upright life. I know that nothing tempting me is unique to just myself; I know others go through the same kinds of things, so help us all."

When we feel like judging others:

Recite Matthew 7:1 "Do not judge, or you too will be judged." (NIV) Then pray: "Father, I'm sorry for trying to take your place as the great judge of life. Please help me to be accepting of the fact that no one, including myself, is perfect. Help me to humble myself where I once would judge others, and instead, use that time to glorify you and your name."

When we need to forgive:

Recite Matthew 6:15 "But if you do not forgive others their sins, your Father will not forgive your sins." (NIV) and pray: "Dear Lord, you are the one true judge; the judge of all creation. It is in you that I seek forgiveness, and I know that I find it hard to forgive _____, especially when they don't seem to be willing to ask for forgiveness, let alone even apologize; but I seek my salvation and know in my heart that unless I'm willing to forgive…how can I expect you, who are perfect, to forgive me? Please put it in me, on my heart, my mind and my conscious being to eagerly forgive. I know I may not forget, because that is part of life (learning as you go along), but please help me to become even more gracious and loving like you. Please forgive _____, because he/she/they are human just as I am and I would like for them to learn to walk closer with you and grow to know you the way that you are continually bringing me to know you more and more each day."

When we face death:

Recite John 11:25-26 "Jesus said to her, 'I am the resurrection and the life. The one who believes in me will live, even though they die; and whoever lives by believing in me will never die. Do you believe this?'" (NIV) and pray: "Dear heavenly Father, I know that through your sacrifice on the cross, all who believe in you are spared the second death which is eternal damnation. I know that anyone who has truly accepted you has a one-way ticket into Heaven, and that his or her name is written down in the book of life. But I still need to have some peace, as this is still a troubling time for me. I feel alone, and I know it could take a long time to get over this new void in my life, so please, Lord, please fill this void with your grace and love and comfort. I need your Spirit to comfort me where nothing else can right now. I need you more than ever so please have mercy and grace and also, bless whoever else is feeling this pain right now."

When we seek to see/love others as God does:

Recite 1 John 4:12 "No one has ever seen God; but if we love one another, God lives in us and his love is made complete in us." (NIV) and pray: "Dear Lord, Please help me to see things from where you view; where all seen is only the truth. I know my flesh deceives me, and this simple fact makes it hard for me to love others the way you love, but I know in my heart that if you would in the least allow me to see them through your perspective, it would make it a lot easier to begin to love them in the ways in which you have called us all to love each other... which is a requirement for us in order for you to be able to dwell within us."

When we need divine wisdom:

Recite Job 28:28 "And he said to the human race, "The fear of the Lord—that is wisdom, and to shun evil is understanding." (NIV) then pray:

"Dear Lord, please guide us with your Holy Spirit. Please give us your divine knowledge, wisdom, and understanding in all things so that we might know how to act in accordance with your will. You say that the wisdom of man is foolishness to you, so please help us to have your wisdom instead. Thank you for what you have already taught us, and please help us to understand even more of your Word as each day passes."

When we need discernment:

Recite Proverbs 15:14 "The discerning heart seeks knowledge, but the mouth of a fool feeds on folly." (NIV) and pray: "Dear Lord, please bless me with an abundance in the Holy Spirit's gift of discernment. Please make me not only wise, but also able to tell good spirits from evil ones, spirits of love from spirits of hatred. Spirits who seek to do harm from spirits who seek to promote prospering love. Please help me to be able to tell when to act, and when to let go...when to heed correction, and when to give it. Please continually bless me with more and more discernment each and every day, that I might be one for others to seek life advice from, knowing myself that the advice I give is that which you would approve of."

When we need energy:

Recite Isaiah 40:31 "but those who hope in the Lord will renew their strength. They will soar on wings like eagles; they will run and not grow weary, they will walk and not be faint." (NIV) then pray:

"Dear Lord, please renew our strength so that we are able to do your will in this life. Please give us the energy we need to sustain our lives and help us to trust in you, that you will be our wings. Fill us with your Holy Spirit so much that it pours out onto those around us. Please, Lord, help us to help each other and be capable of helping each other through an abundance of energy. Thank you for always understanding and in your will we ask this: that we have exactly what we need to remain in your will."

When we're worried about our nation and world:

Recite Proverbs 28:2 "When a country is rebellious, it has many rulers, but a ruler with discernment and knowledge maintains order." (NIV) and pray:

"Dear Lord, please be with our leaders in this time of struggle. Our nation needs more of you, and our world is in chaos. Please help all our leaders act in accordance with your will, only doing that which you approve of. It is by your authority that anyone comes to power, so I pray that in your authority, they act. I pray that all plots, plans, schemes and snares of the enemy be revealed to our leaders so that they might know how to avoid them. I ask of you to fill our leaders with your divine wisdom, your strength, your encouragement and energy. I ask that you guide, direct, surround and protect them with your Holy Spirit, your guardian angels, and your full armor. Have them act only the way that you would approve of and please Father, have them become examples to the world in how to act in a Godly manner. I thank you that we live in a free nation, but I also ask that you not let our freedom consume itself and turn into sin. I pray that you keep the peoples of the world in order with your Word and that you pour out your wisdom and understanding, love and compassion on every inhabitant of this earth so that your peace may be known."

When we're dealing with addiction:

Special note on addictions: Everyone has an addiction (or, addictions) to something(s). Not all addictions are bad. Heck, you could even be addicted to God or just helping people. But it's when an addiction begins (or already is) getting in the way of your wellbeing, the happiness of others, and your relationships with them (including God), that you should seriously reconsider your addiction. Petition Him in prayer. Seek His insight into knowing whether or not your addiction truly is bad; but know in your heart that if it is sinful, and you feel convicted, that it is something you should do your best to overcome. That doesn't mean you have to rid yourself completely of whatever it is that you're addicted to; all that means is that you should at least try to lessen the amount of how much of it you allow into your life. But always keep in mind that if you know it is sinful, it needs to depart from you and rebuke it.

If someone else you know suffers a problematic addiction, please don't try to "throw the book at them" and make them feel defensive, unloved, and ostracized. Instead, win them over with patience, kindness, and maybe even by using yourself as an example. Don't say "YOU need to do this", say, "It would be nice if..." and always bare in mind that no one is without sin, that we all have our faults, and that our purpose in overcoming these is to work together; not against one another. For it is sin which God detests, not the sinner... Lift yourself up, lift others up, and always keep in mind that even though we are supposed to better ourselves daily; whenever we know there's some way we can, we will never be perfect in this life. I know I'm not.

Recite 1 Corinthians 5:9-11 "I wrote to you in my letter to not associate with sexually immoral people-not at all meaning the people of this world who are immoral, or the greedy and swindlers, or idolaters. In that case you would have to leave this world. But now I am writing to you that you must not associate with anyone who claims to be a brother or sister but is sexually immoral or greedy, and idolater or slanderer, a drunkard or swindler. Do not even eat with such people." (NIV) and pray: "Dear Lord, I am sorry for my addictions which have hindered me in the past. Please help me to overcome any worldly addictions I still have, and please help my loved ones as well. I know that you say to be of sober mind, and that is for good reason. I have been selfish wasting my time on worldly things, when I could have been using that time to serve in your kingdom, or simply have been using that time with family and friends as opposed to wasting away in the flesh. I know I can't handle this on my own, nor can my loved ones who suffer with addiction; so I pray and ask that you be our strength; that you be our power, and that with you, we shall all overcome the addictions of the flesh and use our time wisely to glorify your name as it deserves to be glorified. Thank you for being so patient with me, and all of us. I want to seek and depend totally on you, so please help me to."

Afterward

There's no one prayer to cover them all (other than asking God to do His will), so if you need a formulation for how to pray over something not covered in this book, use this formula:

Dear Lord, I have a <u>problem</u>. Please help me to understand this problem the way you understand it. Then, please help to subtract this problem from my life, replacing it with a positive of you.

In prayer:

Problem – problem = 0

0 = void

Add positive to 0 to fill void with God (anything of God is a positive)

Fill void with God = Good prayer

Part VIII
Psalm 23

Psalm 23 (NIV)

The Lord is my Shepherd,
(That's relationship!)
I lack nothing.
(That's Supply!)
He makes me lie down in green pastures
(That's Rest!)
He leads me beside quiet waters,
(That's Refreshment!)
he refreshes my soul.
(That's Healing!)
He guides me along the right paths
(That's Guidance!)
for his name's sake.
(That's Purpose!)
Even though I walk through the darkest valley,
(That's Testing!)
I will fear no evil
(That's Protection!)
for you are with me;
(That's Faithfulness!)
your rod and your staff, they comfort me.
(That's Discipline!)
You prepare a table before me in the presence of my enemies.
(That's Hope!)
You anoint my head with oil;
(That's Consecration!)
my cup overflows.
(That's Abundance!)
Surely your goodness and love will follow me all the days of my life,
(That's Blessing!)

and I will dwell in the house of the Lord
(That's Security!)
forever.
(That's Eternity!)

Afterward

Break down Psalm 23 and use it in prayer. It's widely quoted but rarely used. Use it!

Part IX
Other Forms of Prayer

Dear Lord,

As I set out to read this next chapter, help my brain to be like a sponge, absorbing everything it has to offer, but only have me see things the way you view them so that what I learn is only what you would have me learn. And as I read this next segment, please reveal to me new ways to pray that aren't listed in this book. Spark up my creative side so I can have even more ways of communicating with you and worshiping you.

Writing Letters to God:

Get a journal, but instead of writing it as a normal journal, have each entry be a letter to God. Knowing that it's a letter to God, it's sure to list all of your life's difficulties, but it will also be written in a praiseworthy fashion. This will make it so that when you go to review your "journal," you'll be able to easily count good blessings and how many prayers God has answered. It's also a good way to keep track of your walk in faith to let you know just how you're doing and whether or not you should step up the game a little more and remind you that God is faithful.

Lifting Hands in Prayer:

Think of when cops tell people to put their hands up; it's a sign of surrender, and a sign that they have no weapons. When you stretch your hands out to God, it's showing Him you surrender your will and that you are seeking His will for your life or circumstance.

Fasting

When we fast, we are putting ourselves into a state of constant physical prayer. We are denying the flesh continually, and it is at this time when our prayers become even more powerful. It is always important to pray when fasting, and to fast frequently. Do not use fasting as a means of dieting; use it as a means of prayer and worship to God.

Worshipping

Worshipping God is also a form of prayer. Whether singing praises and songs, or simply telling God you love Him and are thankful for His good graces...it can even be a form of art. Worshipping is a time when you are speaking to God and He will hear your call. Remember, God may not always answer your prayers the way you ask them to be answered, but He always will answer them in His will, the way that He knows how to best answer them. Also, God will answer your prayers in *His* timing. This requires patience on your part, but know that His timing is perfect, whereas ours is imperfect. We must remain adamant even if it feels as though God doesn't hear us.

Listening

Though we might think of prayer as a time to only speak to God, it should also be a time to listen. Be patient, and know that He will respond...whether through word, another person, or another way.

Prayer Chains

Another good way to pray is in prayer chains. Send out an e-mail or letter to multiple people and have them pray for what you request. Or respond to someone else's request by praying for them

Prayer Circles

One of the best ways to pray is with multiple people involved. The more people you have praying with you, the more powerful the prayer will become. Especially when you have very personal prayer requests. The Bible says where two or more are gathered in Christ's name, there He will be, so gather your friends, join hands and pray together.

Phone-a-Buddy

Another great way to pray is over the phone. Pick a friend or friends who will agree with you to regularly pray together over the phone. This is like a virtual prayer-circle, and provides about the same power as joining hands in prayer.

Texting

Send out prayer requests to your fellow Christians using text messaging. Keep it simple, concise, and easy to understand what your prayer request is and I'm sure your friends will be more than willing to pray for you.

Practicing His Presence

Spend a day...maybe even more simply letting God be your main focus. Spend it in peace...spend it in communion. Pray throughout the day, give thanks continually. Worship and praise Him, and sing songs glorifying who He is. Spend moments in meditation; free your mind of life's burdens. Let good thoughts from the Lord come to you, and become more in tune with Him. Let this be a mental vacation…an escape from your usual, to grow in the spiritual.

Afterward

So you've covered just about every form of praying, right? Nope…there's still a limitless abundance of ways to pray and I challenge you to think of new ones. God is eager to hear our voices cry out to Him, but remember, when calling out to God, that it *is God who you are speaking to* and not some random person. Be honoring to God and don't take His name in vain. Be humble when you ask Him anything, having a contrite heart so that He may answer your calls. If He doesn't answer your prayers, be patient, asking for things in *His name* with things that *He would approve of* and I promise you that in *His timing and His will,* your prayers will be answered.

Part X

Closing Prayers

Dear Lord,

Thank you for this book and for giving me the wisdom to understand your will. Thank you for giving us all life in abundance, and for dying on the cross to forgive us of our sins. Thank you for being there for us even when we don't realize that you are, and thank you for allowing us to have a personal relationship with you. I ask that you enter our lives even more than ever before, and that you continue to show us your grace and knowledge and understanding. I pray that you continue to spiritually cleanse us, so that there can be even more room for you and your Spirit to dwell in us. I also ask that you forgive us of all our sins. Please help us to remain forgiving towards others, and help our knowledge and understanding of you span far beyond the reaches of this book. Please motivate us to do your will, and have your will be something that is highly enjoyable to us. I pray and ask that you heal us all, physically, spiritually, mentally and emotionally, and that you guide, direct, surround and protect us with legions upon infinite legions of your guardian angels; with your full armor and with your powerful Holy Spirit. In all these things, I ask that your will be done on earth as it is in heaven. Amen.

Closing Pray From Scripture:

Dear Lord,

"Let it be so now; it is proper for us to do this to fulfill all righteousness." (Matthew 3:15 NIV), and "Jesus answered, "It is written: 'Man shall not live on bread alone, but on every word that comes from the mouth of God.'" (Matthew 4:4 NIV). We need your great Word, Lord. To the enemy, I tell him: "…Away from me Satan! For it is written: 'Worship the Lord your God, and serve him only.'" (Matthew 4:10 NIV).

"Foxes have dens and birds have nests, but the Son of Man has no place to lay his head." (Matthew 8:20 NIV) Make us your resting place. (Matthew 8:20 NIV). "'The harvest is plentiful but the workers are few. Ask the Lord of the harvest, therefore, to send out workers into his harvest field.'" (Matthew 9:37-38 NIV). "For whoever does the will of my Father in heaven is my brother and sister and mother." (Matthew 12:50). I am completely grateful for this. Jesus, you are the Lord, and "Whom have I in heaven but you? Earth has nothing I desire besides you. My flesh and heart may fail, but God is the strength of my heart and my portion forever." (Psalm 73:25-26 NIV). Lord, I pray that you cast the evil out my life and the lives of others (Mark 1:25), and that you quiet all evil. You have forgiven me my sins (Ephesians 4:32). You've asked: "Who do people say I am," (Mark 8:27 NIV), and I reply "King of Kings and Lord of Lords." (Revelation 19:16 NIV). "to him be the glory in the church and in Christ Jesus throughout all generations, forever and ever! Amen." (Ephesians 3:21 NIV).

Afterward

At many times in life, we simply don't know what to pray. It is at this time that we know prayer is highly needed. The enemy is good at confusing us to the point where we feel like prayers are not worth it, or are unneeded. We need to always remain in prayer, throughout all days, all times, and all circumstances. Whether praying in thanks for God's many blessings, asking for hope when we feel there is none, or simply praying just because we feel something isn't right, we need always to remain in prayer, as it is our one true direct connection to God through His Spirit. Pray often and pray when you don't know what to pray. Come humbly before the Lord and come as you are. Earnestly seek him and be diligent in what you ask of Him. When all else fails; pray.

Prayer List:

(Things I need to pray for)

This section isn't meant to replace any prayer notebook you have, but rather, it is for jotting down simple topics you think should be added to this book. Whether it's something that popped up in your mind while praying the aforementioned prayers of this book, or an issue in general that you know you, in your righteous heart, should pray about regularly, keep it simple, keep it general, know that it's important. When the time comes that you've forgotten and can't remember what you've written here, you'll have this to look back to. The world needs prayers, so write small to list as many topics as possible. :)

_____

_____

_____

_____

_____

_____

_____

_____

_____

_____

_____

_____

_____

_____

_____

_____

_____

_____

_____

_____

_____

_____

_____

_____

_____

South:

Order in Chaos
(Revised, Expanded)

God is **ORDER** in this
CHAOS we call life.

Order of the Chaos: (Table of Contents)

How to Use this Book:

Study each meditation and think to yourself how this could apply to your life. Then read (emphasis added) each suggested scripture (either have a Bible handy, or BibleGateway. com) and meditate a bit more. Pray the prayer following the scripture(s), and if epiphanies arise, use the personal meditation space provided to jot down your own thoughts and notes. Use all that you gain in this for the edification of the Body of Christ, to help yourself, as well as fellow believers grow stronger, closer, and more in tune with our Lord and Savior Jesus Christ and His word, and especially for non-believers, to help win them over to the salvation which our Lord and Savior has suffered for us to freely have.

In its "incompleteness", this book is designed to get you to think outside the box. It's been called "thought provoking". Some nuggets of wisdom in it may not matter much to you, because you've already gained the intended insight elsewhere in your life, while others will help you to grow your faith and spiritual intellect even further. Whatever you think of each thought, do so in accordance with what you know God would approve of, and know that it is merely based on questions others have asked me, and thoughts I've had about how to get them (the people who've asked me) to think for themselves so they might one day reach the point of being able to help others in the same way I've helped them. Also, each segment has a name. These names don't necessarily describe how they can be applied, how they can help you or others in your life, or even how you'll see them...they're just names; but I know you'll find a use. To abbreviate this book's title, just say "O, I C".

Have fun :)

RIGHT OFF THE BAT

Imagine your world as a baseball. God's the pitcher and you're up to bat. God can choose to throw the ball in any direction, but when it comes time, you can choose to be prepared through practice and go for a home run, bunt and hope you can "make it", or simply strike out and let someone else take over. When I speak of a home run, of course I mean ending up in the home God has called us to after this life.

Many people wait all across the field of life to catch your ball and prevent you from making it home, whereas God will always throw the pitch right to you. It's just your responsibility to be ready for the right time to swing. Miss it by a fraction and the ball (your world) may not go where you need it to in order to gain a home run.

Suggested Reading
1 Peter 5:8

Please Pray:

"Father, I know the enemy is always roaring around like a lion seeking someone to devour. I know he will always try to throw things at me and make me 'strike out' in this life. So please help me to always 'pick up the bat' and be ready to swing, hitting everything he throws at me and making those things fly as far away as possible; to never return to my life. And please have me always be on the alert for when an obstacle in life is coming, that I might be ready to act in accordance with your will, and yours alone"

Personal Meditation:

ART

Take a piece of art and scrutinize it in your mind. Critique every last detail until you've come to be firm in your judgment of its quality. Now know that even after divulging in all its beauty, you only have a slight glimpse into what kind of person the artist is.

In the same sense, take the smallest bit of creation you can understand, try to grasp how many more of them exist across the universe and then know that even after realizing this, you still only have a small glimpse into how creative God really is.

Add up all the brightest minds to ever exist, and this still would only be a small fraction of the intellect, creativity, knowledge, wisdom, and power that God has.

Suggested Reading
1 Corinthians 3:19

Please Pray:

"Lord Almighty, I know that the wisdom of this world is foolishness in your sight. I know that no matter how much I try to understand, there will always be more I can learn. Nothing compares with your all-knowing, all-encompassing and omnipresent self, so please help me to daily grow stronger in the intellectual ways in which you have planned for me. I pray that you show me things unseen...the way that YOU see them, and gain such insight that I can finally live at peace in trusting in you fervently, no matter how foolish and convincing the arguments of this world might be."

Personal Meditation:

SPLINTER

Take all the pain, suffering, sorrow, heartbreak and tears you've experienced, multiply them by how many billions of people have ever existed and know that all this pain is caused by sin. Now realize that sin is what makes God cry. Even after suffering on the cross, God still endures countless unfathomable amounts of pain because of the sin we humans commit. It's not just a cross that gave him a splinter.

Suggested Reading
Revelation 21:4

Please Pray:

"Lord, you suffer such unfathomable pains that not even the whole of mankind would be able to bear. Yet you promise me that someday you will wipe every tear from my eyes, when there is no more death. I pray that you help me to not sin anymore, and if I do, to catch my sin and immediately ask for your forgiveness and the forgiveness of anyone else I might've hurt. Please help me to stand upright and holy in not just your presence, but in the sight of fellow men as well. And THANK YOU! Thank you SO MUCH for being the perfect one who has chosen to give the ultimate love so that I, myself, might be saved. I love you Lord."

Personal Meditation:

RIGHTEOUSNESS

To be righteous is to walk upright, being noble and wise. To be noble and wise you must have God in you as all things good are of Him. Therefore, to not have God, would mean you're nothing, whereas to have Him, you are something. The better you want to be, the more of God you need.

Suggested Reading
Ephesians 5:3

Please Pray:

"OUR Father, you have called us all to be holy. This seems so impossible with all of our fleshly desires. I pray that you rid me of my iniquities, and fill those voids with your holiness, that I might stand tall in knowing that I no longer have anywhere near as much sin in me as I once did. And please continue renewing in me a steadfast spirit of being the way you've called me to…please fill me with so much of who you are that there's no more room for sin in my life…not even the slightest glimpse of it!"

Personal Meditation:

WHITEWASH

Whitewash is a coating placed over a poorly built building. It is designed to make something look more glamorous and valuable than it truly is. As with superficiality, it is a mere façade and has no righteous place in your life. And as with being superficial: we shouldn't pretend our lives are perfect, but should willingly admit our flaws. But always keep in mind that everyone has problems, and telling them excessively about yours will only add to their own frustrations. If someone is willing to listen, then speak. If you truly need help, ask around and someone will be there. When others need help, use your overcoming of past struggles as an example to help grow others. Never carry pride in anything other than God and the good that He is, and always know that if no human is able to help you with what you're facing, God will.

Suggested Reading
Philippians 4:6; Proverbs 11:14-15

Please Pray:

"Lord God, please provide me with ever greater counsel each time I seek you. Please speak wise words from my lips, and have me hear words of wisdom from my ears. Please show me how to conquer what life throws at me, and use my victory as an example to others you bring into my life. When I need help, please provide it, and whenever any of your children, including myself, need counsel, please have it be readily available at a moments notice."

Personal Meditation:

3rd DIMENSION

Each person in life views things through his own eyes. When more than one person observes any given object, they will always have their own points of view. In the same way, some claim the gospels are riddled with contradictions, whereas in truth, it is merely different points of view to show Jesus in 3D to give us more depth into who He really is.

Suggested Reading
Romans 1:20; John 1:1

Please Pray:

"God, I know my human mind sometimes seems incapable of grasping thoughts of your nature; of who you are. I know that I know not enough. Please help me to grow so strongly in the understanding of your Word, which is part of who you are, that I will always be ready to answer any question that might be given to me regarding it and you."

Personal Meditation:

3rd WORLD

I could've been born in a third world country. We live in the third world away from the sun. Compared to the Kingdom of God; we are in the "third world". No matter how rich, nor how poor; how blessed, or how bright...we all live in a house that God has placed us in. He has designed us to be as one, in the sense of being united through Him, all as brothers and sisters in Christ. So the purpose strives; that we should act as "one", though unique from each other, and not let corruption, greed, and self-seeking divide us. I'm not calling for a "can't we all just get along" type of action; but I am reiterating the point that God wants us to be at peace. When two peoples are against each other, they are as a coin: one person or group on one side, the other on the other, and everyone else caught in the middle as the edge that surrounds the coin. Both primary sides flip the coin to try and "end up on top". Those who surround the coin are what weave it together. They are the foundation of what it means to be humble people, as they know they will never end up on top, but are the mediators between the two sides. Sometimes those in the middle are what the two sides fight about, at others, they could very well cause problems. The point in this is that we should all be moderate with our behavior towards fellow Christians, and always treat everyone else as Christ would, in hopes that one day they themselves might enter the family of God. Ultimately we'll not only grow God's family, but also keep it as one.

Suggested Reading
1 Corinthians 12:12-26; Mark 3:25

Please Pray:

"Father of all creation, please help us to live at peace and resolve our differences through you as our foundation. Please have us always keep in mind that you are our foundation, and that you've placed us all on one rock for a very specific purpose. Please not only have us fulfill that purpose, but please not let us turn away from the Body of Christ, cutting ourselves or others out from it, as a body cannot function fully without it's entirety and overall health. Thank you that you've made us each unique, yet all in your image, and please, no matter what, feed us your Spirit and Word each day; that we might come to grow stronger, more capable, more willing, and most importantly, more pure in your sight."

Personal Meditation:

ENTROPY

Some people think the laws of thermodynamics are "a tough pill to swallow". But let me break relevant ones down to a simple term that can and does apply to your life as a Christian, but first you must think of yourself as a system (your body is, after all, a system of organs).

Zeroth Law - If two systems are in equilibrium with a third, then they are in equilibrium with each other. Think of it like this: If A=C and B=C, then A also equals B. The trinity is like this, in that the Godhead is three in one (Father, Christ, and Holy Spirit).

The 2nd law of thermodynamics states that any closed system is in a state of entropy which will never decrease. Entropy is what we have spiritually when disconnected from God. We are not giving back, and choosing to neglect reception of what God offers. When we are in this state, as long as we remain in it, we are then bound to death; where our lives will reach the third law, which basically describes death, or, "absolute zero". Even if connected to another system (person) and living in equilibrium, all of us humans are finite resources that will eventually die a physical death, and cannot provide eternal life to each other. This is why we need God, as His system will always give life, so long as we accept it. No system is perpetual (never ending or changing), except God.

Suggested Reading
Matthew 28:19; 1 Corinthians 8:6;
2 Corinthians 13:14; and John 5:21

Please Pray:

"Lord, please keep me connected to you, even though no one can truly understand all of what you are. Please fill me with the life you give, and keep me connected to all of who you are. Or else I know I will face eternal death, and that is not what you've called me for."

111

Personal Meditation:

FASTING

Some say we don't need a diet to worship God. Ever consider that fasting is a denial of the flesh, a constant prayer, and that we do it everyday anyway? (Refer to break**fast**). Also, fasting is relying on God to sustain you, which helps us grow our faith. You don't have to fast from food, maybe just from fast food. In this form of prayer and worship, we show God we mean business.

Suggested Reading
Matthew 6:16; Psalm 51:16-17

Please Pray:

"Lord, I know that you do not delight in sacrifices and burnt offerings, but in a broken spirit and contrite heart. Please help me to be of broken spirit, and gain the contrite heart you desire as I deny my flesh; however that is. Each person can fast in his/her own way; so please, when I do, have it be in a way the not only glorifies your name, but also grows my faith. Please help me to deny my fleshly desires by fasting from them in the ways unique to who you've made me."

Personal Meditation:

PRAYER

Amen. We don't need to say amen and hang up on God. If we want God to speak to us, maybe we should leave the phone off the hook and listen all day. Maybe it's wise to pray continually, killing two birds with one stone. If we pray continually, it gives us the opportunity to pray for everyone we daily encounter, while also reminding us that God's connected to our daily thoughts; a way of keeping ourselves in check. (Who would think dirty thoughts knowing God's still listening?)

Suggested Reading
1 Thessalonians 5:16-18

Please Pray:

"Lord, you've called me to pray continually, so please help me to do so, in the ways which are of most help to not just myself, but to all those whom my prayers might have positive impact on their lives. Please enhance my prayer life and help me to understand when it is you trying to speak to me, and not my own fleshly mind, or the words of the enemy. Please help me grow stronger in connection to you, so that others may find delight in my words, knowing that they align with how you have declared they should be."

Personal Meditation:

SCIENCE

Who says string theory isn't just God's voice saying things should exist, and so they do? Who says gravity isn't God's way of showing us we can fall? Who says God, the maker of all, couldn't cram millions of years of dinosaurs and other things into a few simple days or seconds, just so that we'd have oil and even a strong way to challenge our faith so that we can actually prove to Him that we have it? Who's to say that the big bang and/or the universe expanding and contracting isn't just the breath of God and Him speaking things into existence? Who says God didn't set up a system that can govern itself so he can use His time to focus on us? You can't use science to prove or disprove God, but you can use it to look deep into and admire the beauty of His creation. Science is the act of not knowing, while trying to understand. It's continually changing its ideas, theories and understandings of God's creation, whereas our great creator never changes. I like to admire the simple yet complex creation God has endowed us with, but will always give Him credit and praise, as I know He's the one who made it. What does science try to understand? Creation. I like both.

Suggested Reading
Hebrews 11:3; Psalm 33:9;
and Matthew 6:26

Please Pray:

"Lord God, no matter how much man tries to understand your creation, his understanding will always be changing, just as you are eternally creating. Only you know the truth in how all things work. We only have theories and a fraction of your knowledge. Please help us all to see the glory of your creation, and when we find creation's existence hard to understand, please help us to hold strong in our faith; that we do not stray from faith in you - the one who is the greatest creator and creator of all that is good."

Personal Meditation:

SINthetics

A synthetic is something that doesn't exist naturally. It's something made by man. I titled this segment "SINthetics" because all things made by man carry the possibility to cause problems and result in sin. Nuclear research, for example, can be used to provide an abundance of energy, however, we all know what else it can be used for. Pharmacological substances (think: prescription drugs), for example, can be used to help us get over health issues, tame the symptoms of the flu, and do many other great things, but we all know the many side effects that many prescriptions drugs can cause. Sometimes they result in general health problems, to severe disorders...all the way up to even death. The point that I'm stressing here is that: not all things made by man are bad, because many things are good and are used to do great and beneficial things; but it's when the costs outweigh the benefits that they become problematic. If something is purposefully designed for sinful means, then of course its results will be bad. But no matter the case, when you build, design, invent, or even say something, always make sure that it's good, that it will benefit humanity in even the smallest of ways, and most importantly, that it will hopefully aid in the edification and building of the Body of Christ (the Christian community).

Suggested Reading
Ephesians 4:12; Colossians 3:23

Please Pray:

"Lord, please fill my mind with only thoughts and ideas that will result in me producing what will benefit and not hurt the overall Christian community, and also the rest of the world."

Personal Meditation:

TIME

Here's a little tick talk for you: Time is a scarcity that, while constantly being added to, it is constantly diminishing. You have your lot, the set number of days God has allowed for you to be in this life, so use them wisely.

Suggested Reading
Colossians 3:23

Please Pray:

"Jesus, you've existed since the beginning, and yet in the few years you dwelt incarnate, you accomplished more than I have in my entire life. Please help me to use my time as wisely as possible, as working for you, not for human masters...even though they might be my employers. Have all the days of my life be spent wisely and being used to fulfillment, that when my allotted time runs out and you call me home to be with you, that those who knew me in this life might see me as an example to help them do the same."

Personal Meditation:

DEATH

The subject people dread. If you're right with God, you get into Heaven. Yet people still tell me they're scared of Heaven. They say it sounds boring to end up spending all eternity "constantly worshiping God." Who's to say that in Heaven, we aren't just overjoyed to the point where we can't help but saying "Whoa God! That's awesome! You're the best!"

Suggested Reading
Psalm 100; Romans 8:28

Please Pray:

"Lord, whether it's my time, or the time of one I care about; whether it's the thought of death, or the mention of it by someone else...please help me to stand strong in faith in knowing that in all things, you work for the good of those who love you. And for those in my life who have not known you, please help me to do my part in gently showing you to them through how I live, and if I die; how I lived."

Personal Meditation:

A and O

Are some people chosen for heaven, while others are born doomed? I think not. I see God as the Alpha and the Omega; the beginning and the end. Outside the bounds of time where he can see all at once, control all, yet still leave us with our own free will. Only thing is we're tied to a time-line, allowing us to look back on our past mistakes, learn from them in our present, to succeed in our future. God doesn't need this since he doesn't make mistakes.

Suggested Reading
Revelation 22:13; Matthew 6:34

Please Pray:

"Lord, time is something that we can only count, but how can we measure eternity? Please help me to think of the eternal, rather than just the present. To plan long ahead, rather than 'winging it' as days go by. You've said to not worry about tomorrow because today has enough worries in itself, so please help me to not worry, but to still remain prepared for whatever might come."

Personal Meditation:

_____

_____

_____

_____

_____

_____

_____

_____

_____

_____

_____

_____

_____

_____

EVOLUTION

I don't think we came from monkeys, but I do believe in evolution. I believe that God set up a system for nature to govern itself, whereas mankind was in itself most unique of all creation. I believe that He could have created creations till he finally thought "okay, these ones aren't doing it for me so I guess it's time to just make them in our image." Does it matter if evolution is real or not? No. What matters is that we're here, God's real, and we breathe the air He made.

Suggested Reading
Genesis 1:27

Please Pray:

"Lord, it doesn't matter how you set things in motion…the point is that you did. I know in my heart that you've created us humans uniquely to serve you. And No matter how you've truly engineered nature, please help me to always know that it is you who created it. How can a feeble mind of a man grasp the vast concepts of your intellect? Please help me to always see your light in creation, and know that no matter how you did it, it's YOU who did it."

Personal Meditation:

RACE

I believe the diversity of races is just as awesome as how we have many ethnic foods. God simply didn't want everyone to be one color, just as within each color, people have many different faces. Imagine a world with only one race, and soon you'll be bored. I'm glow-in-the-dark white, probably because generations of my ancestors lived in cloudy areas of Europe, whereas some people are darker, and have genealogies that came from equatorial areas of the planet (sunny places). Does this mean one of us isn't human? No, it just means God never stops creating.

Suggested Reading
Revelation 7:9

Please Pray:

"Dear Lord, OUR Father, thank you for creating a world of diversity. Please help rid me of any thoughts of generalities I might have against any one specific ethnicity, because the fact remains that they are still human just as I am; and in being human, they are the uniqueness of all your creation. So thank you for them as well as for creating me."

Personal Meditation:

TIME PARADOX

If God created all things, then how did He create himself? It's simple, He didn't. He's outside the bounds of time and has always been, and will always be.

Suggested Reading
John 1:1

Please Pray:

"Lord, this one's a bugger. It's difficult for our weak human minds to grasp how you're the creator of all, yet nothing came before you. Please rid me of this and help me trust in you, because the fact remains: we are here, and we are your creation."

Personal Meditation:

PARALLEL

Are there parallel universes? You bet! Heaven and Hell. Can scientists find proof of them? Yes, if they deny or accept God, eventually they will...it's their choice.

Suggested Reading
2 Thessalonians 1:9

Please Pray:

"Lord, science is always coming up with new theories and statements...please help me to always know that even if there are parallel universes in the sense that scientists state there could be, that it just means you've created even more creation; all for your glory. If there ever is proof of another universe, then please help me to be thankful that you didn't just get lazy and give up, but decided to keep on creating because you're such a great artist. And no matter the case, please help me to remain adamant in my faith towards you so that I'm secure in my reservation for the one place I seek to live someday: your kingdom!"

Personal Meditation:

BAD THINGS

If God cares then why does He let bad things happen? When I was a kid, my dad let me play with an extension cord...right next to a power outlet. He warned me I'd get electric shock if I touched both ends, but it took me actually touching both ends to understand what electricity was. Sometimes an innocent one suffers...maybe because this will show the guilty "Hey...that person went through all this and me; I'm the one who deserves that and look how I'm living." Maybe things like this happen to get others to change. Maybe God finds someone He loves so much that He wants to take them home with Him and put an end to their suffering. Life is a test for all of us. It's a way for us to prove ourselves to God. He wants to know who's really committed to Him so that He can weed out the good from the bad; all while allowing us the chance to have free will. There's no way for us to every fully understand things, but no matter what, God is always in the works...whether we realize it in the current moment, or years down the road.

Suggested Reading
Romans 8:28

Please Pray:

"Lord, I don't understand even half of the mysteries of this life and why things go the way they do, but please help me to always see your works in them, no matter how long it takes my simple mind to truly see what your complex mind has done."

Personal Meditation:

ATTITUDE

When it comes to how we act, it's pretty simple. We can choose to act in the flesh, causing more problems for the world, or we can act in a Godly manner, being like Christ by denying the flesh. The more we deny our fleshly natures and act as how we're called to by Christ, the stronger we become. The stronger we become in our denial of the flesh, the greater our willpower will be. The greater the willpower we have, the better those great things we can achieve will be. We all know that the spirit is willing and that the flesh is weak - so rely on heart and in spirit to overcome your weaknesses. In doing this, you will achieve far greater results in whatever you set your mind to; so long as you do not let the flesh overcome the spirit. Strengthen your spirit, and your flesh will become stronger. Everything takes exercise, and exercise is to "put into practice". So put your spirit into practice by living its true calling(s) out daily. Overcome your flesh, and daily grow yourself to be even better than you ever thought you could be. Always set your own personal standards of what you expect of yourself above what you know is possible; then when your results come in, more often than not, you'll have achieved greater outcomes than what you would've otherwise expected. Know that nothing you ever do will be perfect, but perfect yourself as your life lives on. And never expect much in return from others, so that when you do receive gifts and blessings from them, they are always something to be appreciated.

Suggested Reading
Romans 12:2; Galatians 5:16-26;
and Proverbs 4:23

Please Pray:

"Lord God, Jesus Christ, Holy Spirit, please fill me with all of who you are; so much of who you are that it constantly pours out onto all those around me. Please keep me even-tempered, well-rounded, and always in an attitude that you certainly would approve of."

Personal Meditation:

HATING GOD?

Sometimes we don't really understand God. Actually, we can never fully understand Him. Even though our brains have over a hundred billion neurons (brain cells) each, just about the same number of galaxies in the observed universe, and even though our brains are the most complex structures we know of in the universe…try to add all the brightest minds in the world up and multiply them by infinity and that mind wouldn't even be able to grasp the complexity of God. So with knowing that, how can we even begin to imagine what He's really up to? Yes, we've all been angry with Him. It happens. Our weak, feeble minds don't understand everything. God says it's okay to be angry, but even when angry, He says to not turn that anger into sin. So take a breather, try and find peace of mind, but know that making peace with God is the only true solution to fix your hatred.

Suggested Reading
Ephesians 4:26

Please Pray:

"Lord, please forgive me for having hatred towards you. I know that I don't know what you're always up to…in fact, I never really can, but you've proven time and time again that you always come through; just not always in the timing or ways that I'd hoped. But I thank you for how you respond, because in the end, I realize it's always better than what I had even imagined would happen. In the end, you always work for the good of those who love you, so please help me to love, and not hate you anymore."

Personal Meditation:

IDLENESS AND PROCRASTINATION

When it comes to how we act, maybe it's not always so simple. Sometimes we like to be lazy like couch potatoes, we like to put things off till the last minute (if that last minute even comes in time for us to finish what we start). An idle mind might be the Devil's playground, but an idle spirit and soul are the foundation to sloth and leads to a future without cause. If we let ourselves drift into a spirit of doing nothingness, then how are we to be ready for when God calls us to work in the ways for which He has prepared for us? Be prepared for anything life may throw at you by living each day to its fullest. When there's good you know you ought to do, do it. When strife and conflictions arise in their time, those who are less prepared will be blessed by your willingness. Willingness comes from having the strength and stamina to make anything seem simple. And to make anything seem simple, you must first get off your seat, step out into moving to where God has called you, and put an end to standing still. Stand up, stand strong, stand for what's right, but never stand still. How are you to go anywhere in life if you never make a move? Yet when you do move, follow Christ' footsteps and walk in His likeness; not pretending to be Him, but acting in ways which He Himself would. In doing so, you will not only be on the path which God would approve of, but will have rid yourself of idleness and procrastination. There is a time for everything under the sun, and rest is good for the spirit and body to heal, recover, recuperate, and revive. Yet always know that when you finally feel rested, it is then time to get up and move again. Never rest for too long, or else you will drift into the state of sloth, which the devil wants you in. Do not become familiar with rest, as in the true meaning of it (think: family) as this tends to lead to being "frozen", inactive, and not taking part in what you are called for. It's not just God who has called you, but it is others who need you...even if you haven't met them yet. When you act in the righteous way, you will see at certain times in your life just who these others are. And when you finally do come to your days of rest and retirement, know that your state of tiredness will be relieved in God's timing, and that you can look back in hindsight, and pat yourself on the back for knowing that you haven't wasted your time under the sun. Do not be proud of anything you have or will accomplish, but be proud that God has used you. Be proud that He has blessed you with the capacity to do great things, and be proud that your lot of time in this world was and always will be beneficial to the glorification of Him and to the wellbeing of those whom you've positively impacted.

Suggested Reading
Proverbs 10:4; Proverbs 19:15;
and Colossians 3:23-24

Please Pray:
"Lord, you serve attentively day and night and without end; loving unconditionally and giving all that we need. Please help myself as well as others to always have the spirit, energy and motivation to do not only what you call us to, but to be how you desire us to be, so that when work comes, and the spirit of laziness begins to consume us, we may rest assured in our hearts that true rest will come as a reward for what to us, seems like a hard day's work."

Personal Meditation:

TURN THE CHEEK?

When Jesus said to turn the cheek he wasn't showing weakness. Imagine him as a super soldier getting interrogated; turning the cheek, and then saying "Is that all you got?" "Kill them with kindness" is another way to phrase this saying. If you return evil for evil, it begets more evil; whereas turning the cheek throws the enemy into confusion, simply because he's the enemy and he doesn't know how to respond to this. If your enemy has no possible means for reacting in an evil way, that only allows for him to lash out in frustration, or God willing, finally be broken and possibly cry down humbly before God as your kindness might just win him over to favor in God's sight by him turning to a lifestyle that God would approve of. And should your enemy ask of you forgiveness, make sure you've already humbled yourself to forgive him beforehand, and reply to him saying, "I've forgiven you and hold nothing against you. The only forgiveness anyone needs comes from Christ...not from me or any other man."

Suggested Reading
Luke 6:29

Please Pray:

"Lord, I know how I want to act. I feel like any other human: that it's 'my right' to strike back, but please give me the patience and peace to refrain, knowing in full heart that vengeance is that of the Lord's. That vengeance is for you to carry out, and not me."

Personal Meditation:

SELF DEFENSE

It's always okay to defend yourself…especially to defend those who can't defend themselves. But it's even better to have such a good standing reputation that others will defend you too. Violence, however, is never a viable option. It should be the absolute last resort when all other options have been completely exhausted, and it should only be used to protect one's life, or the lives of innocent people. The excessive use of force is wrong, and even excessive words in anger are a form of force. Depend on God to protect you…depend on Him for all your life's basic needs. Block attacks using wise words to dissuade them, but never "jump the gun" and be "trigger happy". Instead, promote good; "kill with kindness", and in doing so, you might very well win over the hearts of your enemies.

Suggested Reading
Psalm 11:5; Luke 6:38

Please Pray:

"Lord please help myself and others to know and act as you approve of. Please help us resolve our differences of opinions, protect the innocent, and only allow what's proper to take place. Please keep peace in our hearts, and resolve all conflicts through your Spirit; that we not need to resort to any form of violence in defense."

Personal Meditation:

RESPECT

You can't expect respect without having first given it. We all know to treat others as you would have them treat you; but never expect good favor unless you give it. And even in doing so, never expect it in return. Instead, be satiated in knowing that you've done what is right, and possibly made someone happy. Someday you'll find that it's not money or compliments or anything of this world that will make you happy, but knowing that you make positive impacts on other people's lives. Someday they may return the favor, not to you, but to yet another person. And so a chain reaction is born, and the true reward you may have will be many great people to have as friends when you're living in heaven.

Suggested Reading
Philippians 2:3; Romans 12:10

Please Pray:

"Lord, please help me to first and foremost place you in the highest position of respect as you are the only one who is truly pure. Secondly, please help me to always give respect where respect is due; and even to those who I feel do not deserve it, as I know it will keep the peace and hopefully someday spread like a wildfire."

Personal Meditation:

PEDESTAL

Everyone is born with a pedestal before them…it's their choice on what they wish to have placed there. Whether you choose Jesus or something else, you can only choose one. You can only bow down to one master, as Christ has said, so place no others before God. Make Him your first and foremost priority, but know that in loving others, as how true love is defined in its many forms; you are, in fact, loving and serving God. Also, when giving in any form, always remember to only give what is needed. If you give someone a gift of gold one day, they'll of course be highly appreciative. Give them more the next day, and they'll still say "Thank you." But if you were to give so much that they could buy everything in the world and find no more use for the gold you give them, it really won't mean much to them. They might even come to take advantage of you, using you only when they need, and ultimately, not appreciating you for who you are. This only applies to when you're giving to other people. Give in moderation. Give what's needed, but never in continual excess. That's not to say that an occasional showering of gifts is wrong, because that wouldn't be continual excess. But also remember that when giving to God, nothing we can ever give Him, not even our very lives, could ever amount to equal what He has given us. So when giving to Him, always give your best, your fullest, and as much as you can; because He's the one who will never underappreciate when you give to Him.

Suggested Reading
Matthew 6:24; 1 John 4:19-21

Please Pray:

"Dear Lord, please help me to always keep you as the center of my focus. Please allow me the mental capacity to still focus on what this life requires of me, but to always know that above all, it's YOU whom I serve."

151

Personal Meditation:

ORDER OF OPERATIONS

I'll start with the first companions God made for man: animals. Why I'm starting with this is because if you have pets, and neglect them, then how so would you be as a parent when that times comes (if it hasn't already)? Speaking of parenting and the life around it:

The historical Judeo-Christian value system is basically this:

#1 – God

#2 – Wife (spouse)

#3 – Kids

#4 – All others

And then, by the teachings of Christ, being selfless as He is, it's safe to say that #5 (the absolute LAST priority on your list) should be yourself.

Put all others before yourself, but know the priorities of whom you serve. Don't worry about your own wellbeing, because loving others is loving God, and those who love God will always be taken care of.

Suggested Reading
1 John 4:8; 1 John 4:20-21

Please Pray:

"Lord God, Jesus Christ, Holy Spirit, you are above all, and please help me to always know this in all I do. To the one who've you've blessed me (or will bless me with) to be my companion in this walk we call life, I thank you and pray that I'll be the best to this person that I can. I thank you for my kids (or the kids I pray you will bless me with someday), that they will grow to be so much more than I ever have; teaching them all I can, that they might have a better life than me and not repeat my mistakes. For all others, I pray that you use me as a blessing to them, and lastly, please take care of me, so that I can take care of them."

Personal Meditation:

THREE THINGS

In life, God has given humankind many things, but three stand higher than the rest. Of these three things, if even one were missing, life itself would a) not be possible and b) not be worth living. These three things are:

#1 – Life
#2 – Salvation
#3 – Each other

Without life, of course we wouldn't be here. Without salvation, of course we couldn't live life eternal. And without each other (say: the opposite sex, for example), how would we reproduce and also…wouldn't life get a little boring?

Suggested Reading
Genesis 1:27; John 3:16-17;
and Ecclesiastes 4:9-12

Please Pray:

"Father, thank you for the gifts you've given us; though we're unable to truly know each and every one. Our minds can't grasp the simplest of things you've given us in secret, but the things most important to us, which are all gifts of your unyielding love; I thank you for as life would not be worth living without having them. We need each other. You don't need us, but you choose to keep us and love us. We don't deserve it, but you choose to bless us in abundance…even if we don't see it. Thank you for life, salvation, my spouse (or future spouse) and everyone whom you've created; as all are gifts in their own rite, and every gift from you makes life better. So thank you, Lord."

Personal Meditation:

PROSPERITY

Life is full of times of struggle but it's these times of struggle that carry us through to the true moments of prosperity. They build us up and shape us into who we are. They can be used for our demise, or used for our promotion. They can be compiled into a life that's a mess, or recognized for the truth of what they are: a regular routine of exercise that builds up our spiritual muscle and strength. Occasionally we prosper, but if we persevere, eventually God will grant us true eternal prosperity.

Suggested Reading
Jeremiah 29:11; Galatians 6:8

Please Pray:

"Lord, your ways lead to prosperity. Without you I am nothing, but with you, I have hope. Please keep my sight set on you, and ultimately where you've called me to be. I pray not just that I prosper, but that you bless all those I know with great prosperity and many abundant blessings. Most importantly that with such gifts from you, I pray that we all recognize when it is you who give them, so that your name might be glorified, and no one else's."

Personal Meditation:

DIET

Even though all food is good, it must be taken in regards to your health. As your body is the temple of God, you must keep it clean. This can also be applied to smoking, as smoking is slowly killing you and ruining God's temple. Take all things in moderation. You know when you've filled your needs; so only seek to meet your needs, and know that your "wants" are not of true priority. Seeking what you want rather than what you need not only can and does often lead to selfishness and greed, but seeking only what you need, and blessing others with your "left-overs" may someday be a fulfilling of your "wants". An act of favorable compassion can lead to a life of fulfillment; but self-seeking gratification and gluttony is a form of depriving others of what you know in your heart you could've blessed them with, that they would've met their bare basic needs so that everyone can be taken care of. That's not to say that it's wrong to buy or get a little extra just for the heck of it occasionally, but it is to say that when you know others are in need (which others always are), make sure you've done what you know in your heart to be righteous in God's sight, giving them what you can so that their needs are met, and in the end, share in the excess of wealth that all might be happy. Throw a feast, have a good time…be thankful that God has blessed you with the rare and highly valued position of blessing others. But never seek praise for what you give, instead, if you are praised, remain humble in spirit, knowing that your gifts comes from God, and reply, "Thank God, because without Him, I wouldn't even be able to take care of myself."

Suggested Reading
1 Corinthians 6:19-20

Please Pray:

"God, please help me to be moderate in how I consume things. Please help me to only consume that which is good, and in a portion that is not harmful to your temple (my body). A little bit of chocolate isn't bad; you've created a vast wealth of indulgences for us to enjoy, but please help me as well as everyone else to only consume in the appropriate level of moderation."

Personal Meditation:

CREDIBILITY

It takes a lifetime to build, and in the blink of an eye, it can be destroyed. A man is judged by his word, and in keeping it, he remains who he says he is. In defying it, he is defying himself and the credibility he once had with those he converses with.

Suggested Reading
Proverbs 12:22

Please Pray:

"Lord, please keep my lips from deceitful speech. Yet please help me to refrain from saying anything that is sinful and damaging to others. And when I need to confess, please give me an outlet to do so, where I can be helped to become a more purified person for you. Thank you, Lord."

Personal Meditation:

CREDIT

It's been said to give credit where credit's due. It's also been said to not judge, but to promote the good in people. When someone has a gift, skill, or talent that surpasses the norm, let him or her know it. Even if it's a simple way of how someone is kindhearted or passionate about something that's in-line with God's favor, lift their spirits up and in doing so you will help this person grow and want to grow more in the innate qualities God has given them. When it's yourself to promote…give yourself a pat on the back for doing good; but give all praise to God, for it is Him who has made you able to do the good which you are capable of.

Suggested Reading
1 Thessalonians 5:11

Please Pray:

"Lord, thank you for the amazing people you've created. Thank you that I'm one of them, and thank you for providing me an abundance of opportunities to help others grow in their gifts. Please keep me humble from pride in things that are worldly, but make me proud in you and what you're doing. What you have given and will give…I ask that you give more. Even though I don't deserve this, please bless me with gifts beyond measure according to the abundance of your riches and glory in heaven. Bless me so much so that I can be blessed enough to pour out my blessings onto others, and so much so that when I wake up each day, I'll live with purpose and all those who I encounter will someday (if not already) be living and praying the same way."

Personal Meditation:

ONE WAY

There's only one way into Heaven, and to know this you must know that Jesus is "the way, the truth and the life." The enemy wants you to believe anything else but this, because he knows if he can keep you from true salvation, he'll have you forever away from God.

Suggested Reading
John 14:6

Please Pray:

"Dear Lord, please spread this one simple truth around the entire world. There are many who say there's an infinite way into your kingdom, but you've clearly stated that there's only this one. So please have it be heard, and to those who hear, please provide them with the communion they need; the support of other Christians so that they might grow to truly know you and help spread your one simple truth which is the greatest truth we need to know in this life."

Personal Meditation:

SOCIAL?

What is it to have followers? We are called to be followers of Christ and not followers of mindless ramblings. Though social networks have good qualities, like the ability to connect people, find long lost friends, organize get-togethers, and many other things, they are often used in ways that promote sin, slandering, and things which we all know God wouldn't approve of. Instead of using social networks to bicker about mere splinters in your life, why not use them to promote good relationships and spread ideas that could benefit humanity?

Suggested Reading
Ephesians 4:29

Please Pray:

"God, please help me to always be found good and upright in the sight of man and most importantly: you. Please help me hold myself from saying anything out of rage or anything when I'm not in a clear-minded conscience...or anything which could harm others emotionally. Instead, please inspire me to spread words of encouragement, wisdom, friendliness, and overall, words that you would approve of."

Personal Meditation:

DOMESTIC SURVEILLANCE

You think a governmental domestic surveillance scandal is bad? How about this: God's always watching you and the punishments He can give are far worse than that of man. Even if there weren't any human invasions of privacy (no matter who or where they come from), always know that even the most secretive of things you do, God will see. So always know that even when alone, someone is watching, but that He does it for the benefits of your growth, and overall eternal salvation. Live as though you're being looked over, and with this in mind, maybe it'll be easier to live a more upright, pure, and Christ-like life.

Suggested Reading
Psalm 139:1-16

Please Pray:

"Lord, thank you for always watching over me, but please never let me lose sight of you. I know that you're always looking out for me, and even though I know that it's hard to live the way you call me to…please help me to do so."

Personal Meditation:

SOCIAL SECURITY

We should look out for one another. To whom much is given, much is required. So no matter your gifts; whether they are riches or talents; share them with one another and spread the wealth. Who knows…someday you yourself may come to need help, and someone who you've blessed could very well be your way out. A person you bless with a mere offering one-day, may very well end up being wealthy and prosperous. Your stocks and riches may plummet someday, but if you've blessed enough people, there's no doubt that at least one of them would be there for you when your times of true trouble arrive.

Suggested Reading
Hebrews 13:16; Luke 12:48

Please Pray:

"Lord, thank you for the security in knowing that there are fellow Christians who are eagerly willing to help me, but please help me to use my own unique gifts and blessings to help others."

Personal Meditation:

JUDGING

God is the great judge. He's the one who decides where you'll spend eternity, but he doesn't send you to hell. Only you can choose to go to hell by denying Him. Also, do not judge others, as there is only one judge. Who are humans to judge others when we are all created equal and born into the same sin? The Bible says that those who don't know Christ and haven't heard the laws of God will be judged according to the laws that they do know (read Romans 2:11-16). Not all things are said with words. Mere expressions from your face can have the hugest impact on how others view you and what you mean or how you are. Most people assume things of someone of whom they do not regularly interact with merely based on how they appear and/or what they've heard about them. It is because it's our nature to think only by what we see. But it is what is unseen that defines what is truly inside an individual…his or her heart and how they truly think or feel about life and others. Look through someone's eyes to see who they really are. Think past the flesh and do not be deceived by it, for it ages and may show scars. But as with each scar, there is a story behind it. The story could be of a person acting out of good conscience, or from living a life in sin. But no matter the case, know that what you see is only a sign that something is there…not that you know what that something is. Do not let a mere scar weigh on how you perceive someone. And as with any story you hear about anyone else, or even from anyone else about himself or herself, always know that there are many different perspectives, and none is 100 percent accurate. There is something called the "telephone game", where a group of people sit in a circle, one person starts out with a simple sentence. That person whispers it into the ear of the person sitting next to them, not letting anyone else hear it, and then that person who they've whispered it to repeats the sentence to the person sitting next to them, and this continues from person to person until it eventually comes back to the one who originated it. When the sentence has finally made its way around the circle, back to the one who originated it, they are blessed with proof of how gossip and mere word of mouth can drastically change what was initially said. So when thinking of others, taking all things into consideration, through relying on God: seek only His wisdom and discernment when weighing how you view others. He will offer insight in many forms, but what one man says about another is never filled with the fullness of how God will see that person. We are all flawed in our own ways, so let looks be nothing to tip the scale on what you think. Let no gossip deceive you; but most importantly, look for the good in others and let actually getting to know someone in person be the only way you come to "see" them. Always remember: when your eyes and mouth are set on someone else, you're only drawing attention to yourself. You may not see the attention or the effects of it, but it is there and could very well come back to bite you in a way that causes problems in your life. So hold your tongue, tame your eyes, and see people with a clear conscience. Know that no matter what: no human brain can ever fully fathom another, as it can barely fathom its own problems.

Suggested Reading
Matthew 7:1-2; Romans 2:11-16;
and James 4:17

Please Pray:
"Lord God, it's one thing for me to see how someone's apparent character is…it's another for me to think I have the right to judge them. Please help rid me of the urge to make assumptions about people and even if I know in fact that they are living in sin, please put it on my heart to pray for them, rather than ostracize them. Please help me to help them, rather than say or do something which would only make them fall more into their sinful ways."

Personal Meditation:

ADD

So you think those with mental disorders should be stigmatized? We ALL suffer some inherent flaw, and even autistic savants, even though usually incapable of "normal" social interaction, are EXTREMELY capable at the gifts God has given them. From memorizing complete symphonies and reciting them note-for-note, to memorizing the entire Bible or solving complex problems in a split second. And those with ADD have an ADDed benefit. Take today's news for example. You'll often see many different people all talking at the same time with little letters scrolling across the bottom of the screen called "tickers" which mentioning a vast array of other current events. And someone with ADD can use this "disadvantage" to their benefit, if they learn how to overcome the obstacles it can entail. But when it comes to stigmatizing those with disorders, God says not to do so. Stigmatizing is ostracizing, and just because a very small percentage of affected individuals carry out heinous acts, doesn't mean all with a condition are like that. It's like any group of people; we can't stereotype into thinking one of a group is like the rest, or that all of a group are like one. So don't bully them into having an even harder life. Promote the good in them and help them overcome their struggles they've no control over.

Suggested Reading
Leviticus 18:14

Please Pray:

"Dear Lord, please forgive me for any 'fun' I've made of those who struggle with disabilities. Please help me to be favorable to them, and not a curse in their life. A helpful happiness to them, and not roadblock."

Personal Meditation:

BULLYING

Even if someone doesn't have a mental disorder, everyone has sensitivities about their own vulnerable parts. As an object is only as strong as its weakest point, so too is man. When we bully someone, and when someone is bullied enough, they tend to end up depressed, down, hurt, and angry. This can, and sadly often does, lead to them living a life feeling as though the world hates them; because the world they've known, at least as they've grown. So we shouldn't bully. It makes us no better than those who've hurt us. On the worst side of things, one who is bullied beyond what they are able to cope with could eventually carry out an act of aggression that can be as simple as lashing out irrationally, all the way up to an event which ends up on the news. Events that happen far to often, which never should, yet sadly are occurring in more of a higher frequency than the news ever reported before.

Suggested Reading
Mark 9:42; Proverbs 29:11;
2 Timothy 2:15; and James 2:10

Please Pray:

"Lord please allow me the chance to mend the broken spirits I've given others. If I'm unable to do so, no matter what, please prevent me from bullying again. I understand and know in my heart that what I might see as a simple poking fun at, could really be a stake right through someone else's heart. And I don't want to be one of those who add to the insults which result in someone going down a path you wouldn't approve of. So please cleanse and forgive me, and please bless all those who are mocked."

Personal Meditation:

HYPOCRISY

We cannot and must not live in a way that goes against what we preach. It's been said to "practice what you preach," but I say to live what you preach. Practice might make perfect, but it's not for the actual game. When time comes to act decisively, you must live what you preach to show your word is not only your word, but also your life. I'm not perfect...I'm far from it; and I'll ALWAYS be the first one to admit it. No one on this planet is perfect, and we all suffer from (in the least), the occasional sin. But the purpose of life is to perfect ourselves, mostly by having God do the bulk of the work while we submit and try to do as much as we as humans can actually handle. Admit your flaws when appropriate, but share your knowledge and wisdom when you know it will help. We're here together for a reason, and that reason is to build each other up. To help others, we must first help ourselves. But no matter how great someone can be; there's always someone greater. And greater than all is God. To a point, we've all been hypocritical. So stop it when you catch yourself, but don't think because someone sins that they don't know God.

Suggested Reading
Matthew 7:5; 2 Timothy 2:24-26;
and Romans 3:23

Please Pray:

"Lord, please instill in me a spirit of living the way in which you have called me to. Please rid me of any hypocrisy which I'm unaware of, yet others may see, and please help me to set examples in how I live...examples as you have set for us to follow; living according to your word. And please help others to do the same."

Personal Meditation:

SODOM & GOMORRAH

We might as well call the modern world the land of hypocrisy. It truly is a lot like the Biblical descriptions of Sodom and Gomorrah; that's not to say that there's much good in the world, because there is. But wherever we live, it always seems like we can look across the street, out a window, or just about anywhere, and see sinful ways taking place. Unlike Sodom and Gomorrah, there's no way to really "escape" where we live... so we must deal with it. We're all here for a reason; to shed God's light in this world, so each day that God blesses you with another breath, be sure you use it to thank Him you're still alive, and that as you get ready for the day ahead, be prepared to shine as a true Christian in hopes that others might come to be attracted to the life you live. But live a life that is truly attractive to others, all while still remaining in line with God's commandments.

Suggested Reading
Psalm 23

Please Pray:

"God, thank you for letting me be a blessing to all those around me, and if I've failed to be a blessing, please help me to be one. Please fill me with so much of your light, your Spirit, and your gifts that wherever I go, wherever I am, and in whatever I do, I can be a beacon of your hope to this world."

Personal Meditation:

GUILTY BY ASSOCIATION

Just because you hang around certain people or commune with them doesn't mean you're like them. It doesn't mean you do the things they do. And it definitely does NOT mean you're "them". Though birds of a feather often do flock together, we sheep of Christ's flock are called to spread out into other groups and spread the word. Don't ostracize or alienate people. And if you see someone with a group that looks bad, don't jump to conclude that this person must be like them...never stereotype or judge. Christ himself did, after all, converse tremendously and very meaningfully with tax collectors, sinners, a prostitute, a lawyer...doesn't mean he was any of those. (By the way, I'm not saying any of these people are evil, as all of us are sinners). But be on guard and keep good company, because "bad company corrupts good character." (1 Corinthians 15:33 NIV)

Suggested Reading
Mark 2:15-16

Please Pray:

"Lord, thank you that you can use me to witness in groups where your message might otherwise be blocked, but please keep me and my mind from becoming corrupted. Please keep my character upright, but help me to be as personable and friendly as possible with confidence to uplift anyone you bring into my life. And please have what I say not be my words, but you speaking through me. Please have the words that come out of my mouth do nothing other than bring joy, satisfaction, fulfillment, and ultimately, glorification to you and your name."

Personal Meditation:

THEFT

There is only one kind of sin in my point of view. And this sin covers all sins. Think about this: If you steal from your neighbor, you've committed theft, but if you cheat on your wife, you've stolen her ability to trust in you (as well as her right to be respected). If you lie to someone, you've stolen the truth they deserve. If you murder someone, you've stolen the rest of their life from them. If you worship other than God, you've stolen his due worship. So all in all, any sin can be considered theft.

Suggested Reading
Exodus 20:15

Please Pray:

"Lord, no matter what my sin is, please remove it from me, as far as the east is from the west. Please help me to give gracefully, rather than to steal selfishly. You see all sins simply as sin, and it is sin that separates us humans from you. So please help me, as well as all others on this planet, to rid ourselves of the spirits of thievery and gain the spirit of giving."

Personal Meditation:

FRACTALS

If you've never heard of fractals, look them up on the Internet. Basically, the smaller part of an object strongly resembles the larger parts of it. All living things are fractal to an extent. A trees roots mirror its aboveground appearance, and from the base, to the branches, to the twigs, to the leaves, veins run in the same pattern from the core to the end. In the same way, even our smallest qualities often shine to show the largest of who we are.

Suggested Reading
1 John 3:1-3; Ephesians 2:10

Please Pray:

"God, please reveal to me even the smallest details of who I am. Please help me to polish every good trait you've instilled in me, and to rid myself of any rust or corrosion in my character. Also, as I am but a mere smallest of parts within the Body of Christ, please help me to be as much like the greatest of it, your Son, the Lord of Lords, Jesus Christ."

Personal Meditation:

SIN

God didn't create sin, but He did allow for its existence. Just as darkness is the absence of light and black is the lack absence of color, so is sin the absence of God. Now, knowing that God is everywhere, you'd think that sin should not exist. But know that it is only when we push God out of our lives that sin becomes apparent.

Suggested Reading
Psalm 1:1-6

Please Pray:

"Lord, please leave no room in my life for sin. I know it's hard… it seems impossible, but with you, all things are possible. Please help me to gain a better understanding of how sin can even exist, so that I might come to know how to confront and conquer it, no matter if it's sin of my own, or the sin of others."

Personal Meditation:

EAST TO WEST

When God says: "as far as the east is from the west, so far has he removed our transgressions from us." (Psalm 103:12 NIV) Imagine yourself heading north. Once you reach the top of the globe, if you continue in the same direction, eventually you will be heading south. Whereas to head east and you remain heading in this direction, you will never reach the west, but instead continue heading east. The same goes for heading west. It is this metaphor which some find hard to grasp, but clearly explains that once God has removed your sins from you, they will as far as the east is from the west...infinitely separate.

Suggested Reading
Psalm 1:1-6

Please Pray:

"Lord, thank you from removing my sin so far from me that I can't even see it anymore. Thank you for forgiving me, and thank you that you, who are perfect, are still willing to put up with me even after all I've done against you. I love you God."

Personal Meditation:

SWORD

The Bible says that those who live by the sword will die by the sword, but it also says that during the end times he who doesn't have a sword should pick one up. But what is a sword? It is the sword of the Spirit, which is God's Word. So to live by the sword and to know that you shall die by the sword, be at peace knowing it is because you chose to pick up God's Word that it will be with you till the end.

Suggested Reading
Ephesians 6:13-17

Please Pray:

"Lord God, thank you so much for providing us all with your Word…our 'swords.' Thank you that you've scribed messages that apply to each and every one of us as individuals, continually meaning more each and every time we read them, but that they are also the greatest weapon of all against the evils of this world."

Personal Meditation:

OT

Some say that the Old Testament is useless. I disagree. Isaiah 46:10 states "I make known the end from the beginning, from ancient times, what is still to come..." NIV. (If you don't believe me, read Genesis chapter 5. Take the names listed, Google the English translations of what they mean, and write them down in the order they're listed in Genesis. Then combine their translations into sentence format, with keeping their translations in the same order. Then read the sentence).

Suggested Reading
Isaiah 46:10; 2 Timothy 3:16;
and John 8:7

Please Pray:

"Lord, I know that you've changed your covenant when you sent your Son to be with us, but I also know that all scripture is God-breathed and useful in many different ways. Please help me to know exactly how to use it, while always remembering that only you have the right to cast the first stone."

Personal Meditation:

PYRAMIDS

Some say: "The pyramids were built by aliens." I look at the biblical story of the Tower of Babel, where mankind was one society, trying to be like God and creating the Tower to try and reach him. I think after God cast these peoples around the world and caused the confusion of languages, man still had it in him to build megalithic structures.

Suggested Reading
Genesis 11:8

Please Pray:

"Lord, there are many things in this world and this life which test our faith. No matter what surprises this life will throw at us, please have us know that tests are always to be expected, and that perseverance in faith towards you is what keeps us on the path to your eternal kingdom."

Personal Meditation:

ALIENS

Do they exist? Would it change the fact that we were still created if proof was found? Who's to say that angels aren't what we think of as aliens? Who's to say that God, in all his infinite creativity couldn't create another species out there somewhere just to have more creation under his belt? Why should it matter if they do or don't exist?

Suggested Reading
Psalm 91:11; Matthew 4:11; Luke 1:26;
and Ezekiel 1:15-18 (Daniel's Vision)

Please Pray:

"Lord, it doesn't matter whether or not aliens exist. What matters is that you've created us, and if you have created other species out 'there', then thanks, because all that means is you just kept on creating! And I know that you have angels, that they watch over us, and that your Word has called them heavenly beings. Life is full of mysteries…that's half the fun of it, but no matter what the case is, thank you so much for at least letting me know that your angels watch over us."

Personal Meditation:

CUSSING

The Bible clearly states to let no vile thing come from your mouth. The reason: the words that are vile can be damaging to those who hear them. The language can become so twisted that once innocent words now become vulgar ones, and texts that were once useful in the edification of the Body of Christ can now be seen as vile. Think of how the word gay has changed its meaning, or ass, how it used to mean donkey. Don't cuss if you want to be right with God, especially when talking with him.

Suggested Reading
Ephesians 4:29

Please Pray:

"Dear Lord, please help me to rid my speech of anything derogatory. And please help others to have the same blessing. Thank you Lord."

Personal Meditation:

CURSING

"But, didn't you just talk about cursing?" No. Cursing and cussing are two very different things, while both are for evil works. Cussing is language, whereas cursing is like casting a spell. Think of it this way: If you tell a kid he's worthless and will never amount to anything, you've put a curse on him by making him think he's nothing. Maybe he'll live the rest of his life depressed and feeling useless, when he could have been much more had you not cursed him. So in short, don't curse.

Suggested Reading
Leviticus 19:14

Please Pray:

"Lord, please help me to not cast curses on anyone's life, and please keep others' curses against me from hindering my walk from you. I know they're just mere words, but sometimes they do cut to the core of who I am and cause pain, and I know all people have felt this same kind of pain in at least one point in their life. So please help rid this world of the cursing that seems to be so prevalent in this society."

Personal Meditation:

CHURCH

"Did God really say you have to go?" That question comes from the pit of hell, and death follows it. Yes, God says we're required to go. It doesn't mean it has to be in a building. As long as it's a congregation, in worship, in study, in faith, in prayer, and in alignment with God's Word, then it's church. Keep the Sabbath holy. Don't let any excuse keep you from going to church and worshiping God with fellow Christians. Be thankful you're in a country where you *can* openly worship Him!

Suggested Reading
Exodus 20:8

Please Pray:

"Dear Lord, thank you that you allow me to join with fellow believers in worship and in praise of you. Thank you for these times where I not only learn, but can help. Thank you for the blessings you've given me, and please, as busy as my schedule might get, put it on my heart to honor your day. You're there for me 24/7, so please at least help me to be comfortable to be there for you 1-2 hours per week; and if I'm a regular attendee, then please help me to not only become a more productive member in communion with others, but to also encourage others to join in and feel your presence as fellow believers gather together."

Personal Meditation:

HOLIDAYS

Say the following out loud:

Holy.

Holiness.

Holidays.

I hope this "tricked" you into pronouncing "holiday" correctly ("Holy" + "Day")...not that most of what we call holidays are holy.

Suggested Reading
Romans 14:5-6; Matthew 15:3;
and Colossians 2:8

Please Pray:

"Lord God, please keep us from celebrating what's not important, but bring us to rejoice in communion for you and who your are. For all the things you do, for all that you have done, and for how you continually love each and every one of us, I pray that you keep us focused on why it is that we celebrate what we do and think no ill thoughts about it. Thank you for giving us all so many reasons to celebrate you; not just on Holy Days, but also in every day."

Personal Meditation:

THE LORD'S PRAYER

Break it down, personalize it, use it, and it will work! You can and should pray the Lord's prayer the way He said to, however, these are thoughts I have when I pray it: "God, OUR Father, who is in heaven (higher than us), HOLY is YOUR name. Name above all names, thy kingdom come (You're kingdom will come), thy will be done (YOUR will be done!), on earth as it is in heaven. Give us this day (life) our daily bread (all we need), and forgive us and help us to be forgiving of those who sin against us. Lead us not into temptation to do evil, but deliver us from the evil, the enemy, all his plots, plans, tricks, schemes and snares, for YOUR'S IS THE KINGDOM, POWER, AND GLORY FOREVER!

Suggested Reading
Matthew 6:9-12

Please Pray:

"Dear Lord, thank you so much for providing the most simple of templates in how to speak to you. Please help me to use it, and please help me to spread its usability to others who only think of it as a simple thing people recite only when joined together at church gatherings."

211

Personal Meditation:

PRIDE

Is it good to have? No. When I hear people say: "I'm proud to be American", I think instead, "I'm thankful that I'm American". I could have been born in a third-world country, picking up blood-diamonds, making only a few cents per day. So no, I'm not proud to be American, but with a resounding yes, I'm thankful I am one.

Suggested Reading
Proverbs 16:18

Please Pray:

"Lord God, please remove all pride from me, as pride truly does come before the fall. But please keep in me a spirit of great thanks to you for all the blessings which you have bestowed upon me."

Personal Meditation:

RESISTANCE

Where should this apply? Anywhere the devil is. The Bible says to resist the devil and he will flee from you. If you don't give in to the devil's temptations, then eventually he'll give up. That's not to say he won't try again later, but it will be with a different temptation. So resist him every time he strikes and eventually he'll run out of options.

Suggested Reading
James 4:7; 1 Corinthians 10:13

Please Pray:

"My God, the one and only, please help me to remember just who you are every single time I face a battle in life. Any time I am tempted to do wrong, please remind me of the costs, and even more importantly, of what the reward is for doing what's right. Please help me to triumph over my obstacles with you holding me up, and please, Lord, make it so that one day temptation will no longer seize me."

Personal Meditation:

WALKING

We do it everyday. But I challenge you to pray everywhere you walk. See where your walk takes you and keep praying. Knowing that God is with you, I challenge you to challenge yourself. If you see someone in need, help him or her. If you see someone who needs prayer, pray for him or her. In doing this you will notice your walk is now with God and not worldly.

Suggested Reading
Psalm 84:11

Please Pray:

"Dear Lord, please carry my weight, so that I might carry the weight of others. Please only allow me to be stressed just enough so that I can easily grow stronger in you, while still having a clear enough mindset to take the time to pray for others. And wherever I walk, please have it be on the path you've laid out for me."

Personal Meditation:

PATIENCE

How often do you find yourself spending minutes looking for the remote when you could just walk up to the TV instead? In today's society patience is almost completely illusive. Yet God has been spending eternity waiting for us to walk in *His* will and not our own. Try to be patient in knowing that God still loves you and is always watching over you.

Suggested Reading
James 5:7-9

Please Pray:

"Lord, how do you have so much patience in dealing with us procrastinating little humans? Please help us to no longer procrastinate, but to act decisively when called to, in the way you've called us to, and to have the patience to wait on others, and especially on you, because good things not only come to those who wait; things from you are the greatest of things. You're worth the wait, God."

Personal Meditation:

TALKING TRASH

Makes us trash. To pass judgment on others for how they look is talking trash on God's artwork. To talk trash on how someone sounds is making fun of the voice God gave him or her. To ridicule someone because of anything he or she was born with, in any matter, is making fun of what God has created. You might be one of those kinds of people who laugh at others over things like this (I hope you're not), but know that God's the one who created that person (or persons), and that we are supposed to be thankful and admire His creation that He has blessed us with…not neglect it over worldly ways.

Suggested Reading
Exodus 23:1-2; Proverbs 26:20;
Psalm 101:5; Romans 2:1;
and Romans 3:23

Please Pray:

"Dear Lord, You've created every single person uniquely, and I have no right not speak foul of them. If I do, then how can I not expect others to do the same of me? Please help me to see the good qualities in others, as you do, and please help others to see the good qualities in me."

Personal Meditation:

BEING SLANDERED

There's a reason why the Bible tells us not to gossip. It's one thing to ask how another is doing…whether or not things are all right with them, because we should care about the wellbeing of others. But when it comes to others…even your enemies, there's almost no way to stop some people from slandering, ridiculing, mocking, scoffing and judging you harshly. It happens to all of us, and most of the time the ones who do it, don't have the courage to say what they sinfully believe to the victims face. But when you do hear or are told of someone slandering you; or if they even have the brass to say it to your face, brush it off. Laugh it off. No matter what, do not dignify their sinful words with a reply. Instead, do as God says and pray for them. Bless them. Forgive them. No matter how hard it might seem, turn the cheek, walk away, and know that God will be glorified when you pray blessings upon them.

Suggested Reading
Proverbs 9:7-17

Please Pray:

"Lord please bless those who ridicule me. Bless them with such an abundance of knowledge to know the truth, wisdom to know how to be, discernment to know right from wrong, patience to hold their tongues, and most importantly, surround them with your presence and fill them with your Spirit."

Personal Meditation:

FLESH

We are all born with the original sinful desires of the flesh. It is up to us to deny the fleshly desires, and strive to live the lives God longs for us to live. To deny the flesh is to allow more room for God in your life. To allow more of God in your life is to become more fulfilled and closer to being the Christ-like person He has called you to be.

Suggested Reading
Matthew 26:41; Galatians 5:16;
and 1 John 2:15-17

Please Pray:

"Dear Lord, you denied the flesh all the way to the end...all the way to the resurrection from your crucifixion. I know I'm not strong enough to go through the same, but please at least help me to be strong enough to deny my flesh when it tries to overcome my spirit. And if my spirit is unwilling, please renew it to gain control over my flesh."

Personal Meditation:

FEAR

The devil's favorite card. Do you fear rejection? Do you fear being put down? Do you fear commitment? Do you fear betrayal? Do you fear others? Realize the only fear you should have is the fear of the Lord! Know that He unconditionally loves, but always carry the fear that if you step out from His will, you can incur His wrath.

Suggested Reading
Proverbs 9:10; Isaiah 41:10

Please Pray:

"Lord, please instill in me only fear of going against your will, and to not hold onto any other fear that this world will try to throw into my mind. With you as my up lifter, my comforter, my protection, my rock and my shield, I know that all I have to fear is you…so please keep this in my mind at all times so that I have the courage to carry out the good deeds which you have called me to, no matter how scary the world may make them seem."

Personal Meditation:

CORRECTION

It is my own personal belief that anyone who ignores correction is either too lazy or selfish to make himself into a better person. We daily can find ways to correct ourselves. We can always be on the lookout for how we can better serve God's Kingdom and we can always accept correction with a big smile. If we don't, then we must think we're already perfect...and we all know that's wrong.

Suggested Reading
Proverbs 12:1

Please Pray:

"Dear Lord please help me to heed correction when it is needed, and to help others correct themselves gently and with patience. No one in this life is perfect, so please keep that in my mind. And please only allow me to become a better person; never a worse one."

Personal Meditation:

FIRST TO LAST

We all know that God's Kingdom seems to be "upside-down," from ours, but know that if you're in the back of the line, you can be first to get seconds.

Suggested Reading
Matthew 19:30

Please Pray:

"Dear Lord, thank you so much for having a kingdom that is the polar opposite of this world...because this world is filled with far too much corruption, greed, filth, sin, anger, hatred, betrayal, and ugliness. Please help me to live as if I'm already in your kingdom...worthy of being in your kingdom. And please help me to clean this current place I'm living in the best that I can."

Personal Meditation:

SOBER

How can anyone justify not being sober when it impairs his or her walk with God? The Bible says to be of sober mind. So be it! Even if your crutch is smoking cigarettes, are you really going to let that little cancer-stick control you? This is not to say that a moderate drinker (social, yet controlled who does not give in to drunkenness is in sin), after all, Jesus' first miracle was turning water into wine. But all things should be in moderation, unless you know them to be harmful to your health and/or over all wellbeing. Yet I personally believe in remaining completely sober as it prevents me from going down the spiral of addiction.

Suggested Reading
2 Corinthians 7:1

Please Pray:

"Lord, no matter what addictions this life might have for me, please have you, serving you, serving and loving my family, loving others, and being an upright person be my addiction."

Personal Meditation:

ALCOHOL

It's not a problem to have an occasional drink…even a glass of wine can help spark up your immune system, but the way society encourages drinking as a crutch for all of life's problems and trick you into thinking it's a good time is a lie straight out of hell. This segment is for those who feel convicted in their hearts and minds for excessive drinking; for those who drink more than they know they should and know that they can't be one of those to "slow it down" to an acceptable, non-problem-causing amount. When I used to drink, I thought it'd cover up and rid me of all my problems, but then every time the alcohol left my bloodstream, I'd realize all the problems I tried to ignore were still there; only often times, a lot worse. One day it dawned on me that the whole "3 Month Rehab" thing had a point to it; even though 8 months in rehab never did much for me (other than provide me with a moment of sobriety and a chance to learn and understand the struggles that other people go through; and that even though they're so different from me, we all shared a same common addiction). But I realized the programs have a 90-day contract for a reason: it's on average, that after the ninetieth day your brain literally "resets" itself. You wake up feeling new, refreshed, reborn, and with a high on life through a clear mind that you could never have with alcohol in your system. Your brain literally gets supercharged. But I still knew there'd be that whole constant bombardment of temptation that the enemy tries to throw at you. Billboards with hot girls; advertisements showing a "good time"; alcohol brands showing all the so-called benefits all while neglecting the negative things that these lifestyles often and usually do lead to. All of the embarrassing things you don't remember, but get reminded of the next day; all the relationships it ruins; the financial problems; and sadly, for a lot of people, serious illness and even death (not to mention the deaths of those who one's drinking can be a result of). So I thought,

"Hey! Alcohol and I...we spend so much time together she's practically my girlfriend." After that I knew I'd have to do the same thing I did to get over any unhealthy relationship: STOP THINKING OF THE BENEFITS AND ONLY THINK OF THE NEGATIVES! It's easier this way. When you do it enough, then every time you hear, see, smell, think or talk about alcohol...if you've reminded yourself enough about the negatives, they'll always pop up in your head when alcohol tries to lure it's way in there. And lastly, there's the third and most important step. We all know that the spirit can be willing but that the flesh is definitely weak. That's why we have to call on God. Humble yourself and contrite your heart. Get on your knees and BEG Him to deliver you from this problem. Ask Him to make even the mere thought, smell, taste, or mention of alcohol make you want to regurgitate your guts out. Ask Him for the willpower to carry on and fight. When you see something promoting alcohol, laugh and think to yourself, "That garbage...thank God I don't fall for it anymore." Be glad it's gone...even if you relapse. And if you do relapse, don't quit the fight. Break yourself and do what you know you have to. Rid yourself of anything and everything that promotes it. Get back up off your back and stay in the fight. Most importantly: hate everything about it and never love it again. Realize that it's not for you. In one, or two, but definitely three tries you'll make it. All you have to do is break your pride and submit to God. No one else can save you except Him. And to have Him save you, first you must humbly submit. So if you have this problem; even if you're not willing to admit it to others...God already knows and so do you. So be proud that there's a way out. Be proud that the God who loves you, who created the entire universe but still takes the time to forgive you and deliver you will always be there for you. Whether or not He answers you in your timing or not doesn't matter, because His timing's the only one that works. Know that in all things, God truly does work for the good of those who love Him. So love Him, hate alcohol, and praise God that you're still alive. Note: Change the word "alcohol" with anything that overcomes you negatively of which you can't control or lessen the amount of. This is only one of many strategies to conquer one of the flesh's weakest sins. But no matter what, always know that God should always be the main point of refuge for all needing help, while still keeping in mind that we must do our own work to achieve what we aspire to.

Suggested Reading
The topic above, every time you need a reminder; and Proverbs 20:1

Please Pray:

"God, you are above all and all things good come from you. I know that for my benefit and also the benefit of others that I need to stop my addiction. Please bless me with the willpower to overcome it; the patience and motivation to know that even if I fail, you will someday deliver me; and most importantly, that when you do free me of this addiction that you put it on my heart and mind to always get sick at the mere thought of it so that I never return to it again. Thank you Lord."

Personal Meditation:

LUST

The big one in life. Whether it's lusting after a celebrity, or lusting after an object; it's still wrong in God's sight. When the Bible says to remove what makes us sin, I see this as: If you're addicted to porn, toss out your computer; if you want your neighbor's wife, move out of town; if you can't handle it, confess it to a fellow believer. Just do what it takes to have thoughts that God would approve of. And remember: desire turns to lust; it begins in the heart and mind. Remove yourself from it.

Suggested Reading
Ezekiel 6:9; Mark 9:43-47

Please Pray:

"Lord, I know it's alright to like something, but please never allow me to get to the point to where that liking becomes lust, because lust is the sin that can cause an entire spider web of problems in not only my life, but the lives of others. So please rid me of the mere possibility of even being able to lust, and please help me to know the difference between liking, lusting, and love."

Personal Meditation:

LOVE

God's favorite word. I know it must be since God is love. All things good are of God, yet the devil wants us to believe opposite of that. True love is truth of God: living God's Word, living on the path he has for each of us, and living upright in obedience with His will. It is true that all you need is love when you realize that love is God and God is love.

Suggested Reading
1 John 4:8

Please Pray:

"Dear Lord, thank you for loving me, thank you for loving unconditionally, but please help me to know and understand the different kinds of love, and how to appropriately apply them to my life, and to only do so in ways which you approve of."

Personal Meditation:

FAITH

Though we've all heard that the faith of a mustard seed is enough to move mountains, how can we increase that faith to move mountain ranges? It's simple: ask God to increase your faith; but be forewarned: the devil will try to keep you from growing stronger (=spiritual attacks). When thinking of the word "mountains", replace it with the biggest of burdens, hurdles, boundaries and obstacles in your life.

Suggested Reading
John 14:13; Hebrews 11:1-31

Please Pray:

"Lord, please help grow my faith exponentially to the point where I no longer have any doubt in you whatsoever. Please help me to understand just what faith can do. Help me to see the works of faith and how they help people. And please do not let me be fooled into thinking the false teachers who cause harm in this world are doing so by faith in you; for I know better, in that they worship a false impersonation of you."

Personal Meditation:

BEING USED

It isn't really a bad thing if it's God who's using you. However, the most dangerous prayer you can pray is to ask God to use you. I guarantee it! Try asking Him this and see just how far He takes you. Asking God to use you might be the best prayer you can pray.

Suggested Reading
1 Peter 2:9; Psalm 116:16

Please Pray:

"Dear Lord, please use me. Please use me to do your will in this world and use me to impact others lives in such good ways that they see it's you in me who does these things, and not me. Please use me in whatever ways you see fit, and never let me be used to cause harm."

Personal Meditation:

SOLA SCRIPTURA

Latin for "Scripture Alone". I personally believe that with all men being fallible, imperfect, and nowhere near close to being who God is, why should we take every single thing one man says and allow it to change our own faith in God? The Bible says to "test the spirits," so do it! Listen to what all your instructors and pastors/preachers/ministers have to say, but ALWAYS check to see that what they say aligns with what God says. (Refer to His Book!).

Suggested Reading
2 Timothy 3:16; 1 John 4:1

Please Pray:

"Lord God, your Word is the living Word, and it carries so many meanings...many being word for word literal, others being metaphorical. Either way, your Word speaks truth to each and every person who seeks it. It speaks uniquely to every person as it applies to what he/she is going through. And I thank you that you've given this world your Word."

Personal Meditation:

UNDERSTANDING

Understanding what God wants us to do can seem like an unsolvable mystery at times, but I want you to know that asking Him to show you is the first step. If all else fails, then just live life according to His Word and you will be in His will.

Suggested Reading
Psalm 25:9

Please Pray:

"Lord God, please help me to understand you as far as I am capable. And if I need to be made more capable, then please do so, so that I might better serve you and grow to understand you even more…you unsolvable mystery!"

Personal Meditation:

TRUST

Seems impossible to have for people, but trusting in the Lord is always a worthy task. You might find yourself in a lack of trust in God, but always know that, however bad life seems, in all things God works for the good of those who love Him. Do not place all your trust in any person, as we all fail eventually even if in the smallest way, but try your best to always give the benefit of the doubt, as long as you are capable of doing so.

Suggested Reading
Proverbs 3:5-6

Please Pray:

"Jesus, please help me to trust in you at all times. Please help this trust to pay off, so that in living a life while trusting you, others might see the benefits of doing the same. And please remove any and all doubt in you that I might have."

Personal Meditation:

GIFTS

It's my firm belief that when God gives to us abundantly, he expects us to share the wealth. How much of whatever could you possibly need that you don't have enough to share? Whatever God has gifted you with, put it to use in His Kingdom. Whether gifts of ministry, or gifts of wealth, give back to God and I promise you, He will bless you even more.

Suggested Reading
1 Corinthians 12:1-11

Please Pray:

"Dear Lord please bless me with all I need, and when I have an excess, please bring the right person(s) to me so that I may help them enjoy your blessings, bringing them to possibly come to glorify your name."

Personal Meditation:

THREE IN ONE

How can God be three unique persons (Father, Son, Holy Spirit), and yet still be one? Water can be liquid, ice, and steam, yet it's made of the same elements. Who are we to question God? We are, after all, created from dirt.

Suggested Reading
Matthew 1:23

Please Pray:

"Dear Lord God, Jesus Christ, Holy Spirit, thank you for being who you are. Thank you for letting me know that you come in many different forms, because each of your forms serves a unique purpose. I thank you for allowing us humans the ability to come to know you."

Personal Meditation:

DEPENDENCE

We depend solely on God for anything to work right in life. It is through God that all things are possible, and without Him nothing can exist. To have more possibilities in life, we must have more of God in us.

Suggested Reading
Psalm 62:7

Please Pray:

"God, please dwell within me even more, in all your forms, that my possibilities of doing great works in this life might be enhanced and ultimately, your name be glorified. Thank you for the possibilities, which you've already bestowed upon me, and thank you for any and all surprises, which you have in store for my future and for all your humble servants."

Personal Meditation:

FORGIVENESS

How can anyone expect God to forgive if they themselves are not forgiving? How can we be forgiven if we still act in a way that needs forgiveness? If we don't forgive those who wrong us, then we can't expect forgiveness for our sins.

Suggested Reading
Matthew 11:25; Colossians 3:13

Please Pray:

"Dear Lord, please forgive us of all our sins. Please help us to all be completely forgiving and please help us to all live more without sin each day."

Personal Meditation:

DENOMINATIONS

There is only one true path to salvation, and that is through our Lord and Savior Jesus Christ. There is no other way to God except through Him, and this is why I don't understand denominations; they didn't even exist when Paul began spreading the message of Christ. The true body of Christ isn't solely Presbyterians, Baptists, Evangelicals, or Pentecostals, no; it is a unified body that transcends all denominations to those who accept Jesus as the only way into heaven, and solely obey his teachings (Christians). Meat is for the mature and milk is for the adolescents in faith (1st Corinthians 3:2). Regardless of pharisaical arguments that divide the church, to be a true Christian requires having the foundation in knowing that 1) Jesus is the way, the truth, and the life, 2) We must repent and be baptized, and 3) We must live day by day, bettering ourselves to be as Christ-like as possible. Strength comes in numbers; so don't let miniscule interpretations divide you from your siblings in Christ. Instead, find common ground in knowing that you all serve a purpose, and through patience and understanding, talk peacefully about your differences of opinion, all while knowing that a church is just a building, whereas it's members should be the builders.

Suggested Reading
John 3:16-17; Acts 11:26; Luke 11:17;
Romans 12:18; and Titus 3:9

Please Pray:

"Dear Lord, Jesus, you are the head of the Church, the Body of Christ, and I pray that you unify all true believers in communion that we might stay stronger together, as there are only few of us. Please stop this dividing of your church, and unify us through you, and your truth alone."

Personal Meditation:

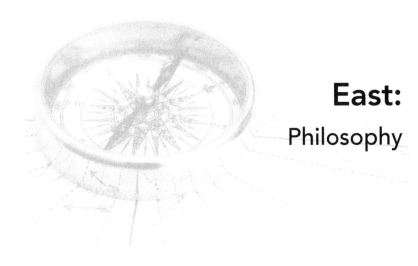

East:

Philosophy

A quick note: If something in here is too complicated to understand, don't worry…it's not your typical philosophy book. If you find something difficult to understand, read past it and keep on reading…there is simplicity in this book. If not in one section, then in another; but I strongly encourage you to read through the whole thing.

Contents:

Introduction: Gnosis

*"Yet these men slander whatever they do not understand,
and the very things they do understand, by instinct-as irrational
animals do-will destroy them."*

– Jude 1:10 NIV

In life, knowledge is knowing, wisdom is understanding, and the future is uncertain. Looking back to the past to absorb the present for an understanding of the future only brings us to one thing: knowing that the past is knowledge, the present can have wisdom, and the future is uncertain. However, when in retrospect we realize how little of any knowledge or wisdom we truly have.

The Bible states: "For the wisdom of this world is foolishness in God's sight..." (1 Corinthians 3:19 NIV), and to God this is correct, but to us, we must address this concern by eagerly seeking to have the wisdom and knowledge of Him who created us. Though our brains will never amount to the sophisticated complexities that run through God's consciousness, we can daily ask Him to show us how to see things from where He views, to see only the truth and to become enlightened towards knowledge of the better paths in life.

We were created with an innate ability to learn and absorb things far more superiorly than any other of God's creation. We were crafted with instinct but were carefully drawn in *His* image to, over time, become like Him. We are to study His Word, delve into its meaning, learn by experience, and have spiritual cleansing. We are to love one another, spread the news of *His* love, think thoughts just as God would and someday, spend eternity with Him.

And so it begins...a big question mark as to where this book is going. It's not where this book leads that you must go; it's where the thoughts God will place inside you must dwell. To enter a state of realization that we truly do know nothing and that we must become fully dependent on God to fulfill our innermost necessities. So reach your true self-actualization, know your true limits, but grab hold of your full potential. It's about time we stop asking "how", and step up to act now. This book is merely thoughts of a fallible human being, and is not designed in perfection. Rather, it is its imperfection that is geared to open your mind, and expand your life. For those who think they know everything are closed to learning anything new; but those who feel as though they know nothing are open to learning everything.

Part I
A Blank Slate

"Yet you, LORD, are our Father. We are the clay, you are the potter; we are all the work of your hand."

-Isaiah 64:8 NIV

We are born without knowledge, but are born with instinct. Instinct. Just as how God instructs the animals of nature to eat, hunt, and do what is necessary to survive. At the same time, I personally believe we as a species are born inherently unknowing. Do not be offended by this statement, but I have come to believe that common sense isn't common. Simply look around the world and you'll begin to notice that some twelve-year-olds are more mature, intelligent, and better gifted than the average fully grown adult, as the average fully grown adult is the exact antagonistic part to maturity. This is not to say that all people are mentally incapable of being mature, or that we are not the smartest of species; it is merely to point out that we could be so much more than we currently are. And this will remain true throughout all the days in which God blesses us to live in this life.

We are as a blank slate in the beginning, with an overwhelming eagerness to obtain knowledge. Yet it is this very eager act of wanting to absorb information that can also be our downfall. As a canvas is open for the artist to paint whatever he or she feels is necessary, we are like canvases, awaiting the colors with which the artist will use to define us. We are dry, simple, and void of definition in the beginning, and every stroke of the brush that touches us gently and sometimes not so gently, shapes us into whom we will become, post-adolescence.

God, as the master creator of all, is who we should have as our artist, painting us continually to become more beautiful in His sight, and more capable in ours. And though we all are created equal yet unique, others can rub some of their wet paint onto us, as it were, having us absorb their likeness.

If this is confusing to you, just think of it this way: there are many people in the world that paint, but they don't paint as flawlessly or without sin as God does. God paints perfect pictures, where man and the enemy paint vulgar, sinful, and distorted perceptions of reality. What God paints, man stains.

When God paints us, we can rub what He paints onto others, helping them to become "fulfilled", while at the same time, others who have been painted by anyone other than God, can rub onto us and infect our overall image.

We all have flaws because we all know not enough to be perfect. If there ever were one perfect human living today, I'm sure he could change the world if he wanted to, but would have a hard time surviving because of the lack of perfection in this world. Others would become jealous, spiritually-carnivorous, hateful, and out-to-get this individual, trying to bring him to demise so that they themselves could take his place and corruptly inherit the wealth which the world would see fit to offer him. I'm simply stating the point that even if we could become perfect in this life, the corruption of the world would lead us to eventual downfall. It is my strong belief that we are not perfected until we enter God's eternal kingdom, where Jesus himself would finish us off and "put the cherry on the top".

Instead of perfection, this world is smothered in a mud of disgusting imagery, residual sin, vulgar language, unequal treatise about faith, and multiple religions, where in all of which, only one can be true.

The main point is that with all this imperfection in the world, you can see why it is that it can be easier to have mud rubbed onto your canvas when really, we should have God's goodness making us who we are. And though God is everywhere, so too is sin.

Even with the occasional genius being born, knowledge does not mean wisdom, and most of us, even if born with overwhelming knowledge, have a complete lack of wisdom unless we seek to have it burned into our inner-being. We often end up getting into trouble, either starting with our parents, or when we become teenagers, and as it is becoming more common than common sense, many adults are losing morality and instead choosing to be offensive, obtrusive, and abusive. There is a lack of freewill for the better parts of our psyche to live in, since the common practice nowadays is to sin, love sin, and love anything but what is truly good as defined by God's Word. In this, true common sense has become rare, and what many think of as common sense, is now just common non-sense. And this is where I believe most of the world's population resides.

It would be nice to see the world through rose-colored glasses in a perfect state of bliss, but deep inside you would still have an understanding that once you remove those reality-defying glasses, life is truly the opposite of the ignorance society tries to make you believe. Things aren't perfect; money is scarce; helping one another has become odd, and even the act of opening a door for someone is something that is now seen by most as just flat out weird. I don't know if this is how life is where you live, but when I get up to leave a chair for a woman, child, or disabled person, a selfish man will rush to take it. To me this is wrong, and is a primal example of the underlying problems which society has. The fact that rudeness is more acceptable than being a gentleman…it just doesn't make sense to me. To me, being a man means living a life God would approve of: treating others as you would have them treat you; of course, while knowing that you should never expect such sincerity or favor in return, so that you are not let down should you not receive it.

I know not all of us humans are morally corrupt, but it seems to me that society is degrading exponentially to the point where no matter where you turn; a negative influence is always awaiting your canvas to rub up against it. The devil wants all resemblance of true perfection wiped off the face of the earth and to do so he must corrupt people piece by piece.

So as we are now not blank slates as when we were born, we are still unfinished products, which have the potential to be corrupted. My point is not to become depressed thinking there is no hope; on the contrary, I believe that with God, hope thrives. We must have on our full armor of God and ensure that none of the corruption, whether it's like how I described earlier or another variant of it, ever touches our "canvases".

So to lead into the next chapter, I hope this wasn't too confusing, but confusion will be the next topic discussed.

Part II
Confusion and Love

"To say of what is that it is not, or of what is not that it is, is false, while to say of what is that it is, and of what is not that it is not, is true."

-Aristotle

This quote from Aristotle might be confusing, but it's simple: what is, is, and what's not, is not. Changing "is" with "not" makes it void. But this is not the focus of this part of the book. What is the focus is that confusion remains as one of the reverse-cornerstones of life; a happening that occurs every time our brain is unable to fathom what is said or what we cannot make sense of. Bible verses are more often than not, very confusing to most people, as is miscommunication. While the Bible remains a series of books not in miscommunication, but in symbolic terms, which either applies to your life, or applies to the life/lives of others.

There are many instances in God's Word where one can become utterly confused in trying to decipher the overall meaning. A prime example is John of Patmos' "Book of Revelation". As it stands, the *Book of Revelation* is riddled with symbolism, metaphors, analogies, and then of course a few things that are straightforward (like not taking the mark of the beast so that you don't lose salvation). It is a very dangerous book to read if your faith is still in its infancy, because it can cause you to think in literal terms where the beasts described are seen as literal translations in real life, when really, as most would agree, they're symbols for kingdoms, tribes, the antichrist, etc. When God's Word states to "Love thy neighbor as thyself", it's pretty straightforward. It means to love your neighbor, yet some would twist this meaning by imploring that they do not love themselves, so they don't have to love their neighbors. Thankfully, the Lord makes it clear to love everyone, by repeating the word love in many other verses (ex: love your enemies). Now, this does not mean you have to be in romantic love with them. No, the definition of love in this world has changed from what it meant when scribed into God's Word.

There are exactly four kinds of love: agape, eros, philia, and storge. Agape is the unconditional love that God has for us, eros is the intimate love that we are to have with our spouse, philia is the love we are to have for friends, neighbors, and enemies, and storge is the love described for family. Storge is probably the most tricky of loves, as coping with family is not something that is nowadays commonly seen as a form of love, rather, it is seen as a duty, requirement, or obligation of sorts.

Many would define friendship apart from love, when in reality, being a friend is the act of loving another to the extent that you feel as though you are siblings. And this is what leads to the main point in topic of this part of the book: that love can be confusion, while it is meant to be that which describes a certain aspect of life, which we are to work for.

I personally have come to believe that in our committed relationships (ex: with the one we marry), we are to not only have eros, being intimate with each other, but are to also try and have every other form of love, ultimately coming as close to having true agape for each other as humanly possible. And though there will be many burdens and obstacles, that doesn't mean we just lose our love. After all, some arguments in relationships are actually rather healthy and necessary for true happiness, comfort, and freedom to exist within the bounds of matrimony.

To note a form of love which is not truly love, but instead inherently evil in the act of having it; the love of money and/or possessions is the root of all evil (money and possessions in and of themselves are not evil). I also believe that no human, not a single person in this world is inherently evil...they just do evil things (set aside those suffering severe mental illnesses; they can't necessarily control all they do, think, hear, feel, and say, so who are we to judge them; when rather, we should help them become healthy).

When I think of loving others, I think of being as selfless, humble, caring, understanding and discerning as possible, while always helping them to make it through this life as best as I can. I don't believe we are required to go so far out of our ways that we must sacrifice all we have to assist others in facing the challenges life brings to them; rather, I know that we must simply do what we know to be right and what God calls us to do.

So with a simple explanation of how I personally have come to know love, you can easily understand just how confusing a concept and emotion it truly is to grasp. I don't believe humans can ever love so unconditionally as to not sin, hurt others in some way, shape, or form, but I do believe that when we try our best, to not only be our best but to love our best, we will reach as high as life permits. And sometimes confusion is what makes love possible. The simple thought of not knowing what to expect, not understanding what to do, being so lost in an unfathomable cognitive and emotional struggle...I think that's what drives us to contemplate so thoughtful the course of action which we should take.

I believe confusion can be its own thing, whereas all love will always have confusion tied to it. Some love is easy to understand, whereas other forms of it, and all the variables which pertain to them...maybe they're just not meant to be understood. Maybe it's confusion that allows for the human psyche to expand its knowledge to the point of true genius.

So what should we know about true love? The word "know" comes from the Greek word "gnosis", meaning, "to know intimately". When Adam came to KNOW Eve, she bore Cain and Abel. So in a logical sense, to truly know someone, is to be intimate, and to be intimate, is to have eros. To have eros, is to have the strongest of human loves possible (just keep in mind that promiscuity corrupts, deceives, hurts, and destroys true eros; so keep it to one person; but love others as much as you possibly can...just know that you can't "know" them in intimate way).

I could go on forever about love, because to me, it's what drives my life. After all, it's God's love for us, which leads Him to bless us so abundantly in the ways, which He does. It's our love for each other that drives us to do good things. It's love, which comes from the heart, which we all know is the well-spring of life. And without love, I just can't see life existing at all.

So grab ahold of the heart God gave you, let the love pour out and know that even if you feel confused, you're not alone. None of us can ever fully understand just how far this word, act and emotion go. And none of us will ever know truly just how much others love us, that is, until we learn how to love the ways in which they do to us.

Part III
Words

"A powerful agent is the right word. Whenever we come upon one of those intensely right words…the resulting effect is physical as well as spiritual, and electrically prompt."

-Mark Twain

Words. Some estimates are that there are roughly 4,000 new words added to the English language every year, and then there's the fact that words can and do change meaning frequently. Many words start out with humble beginnings, and then are eventually altered to mean something derogatory; while others are shortened, and even combined into Internet words like "LOL". They can be used to uplift, they can be used to demote. They can be used to support an argument, and even be used against it. The same words one uses for one purpose, someone else can use for another. And the same thing can apply to God's Word, even though God's Word cannot change and will never pass away (Matthew 24:35). Some people try to twist the meaning of God's Word to delight the "itching ears" of this world, while others use it for its true purpose, which is to help mankind on his journey through life; growing closer to and glorifying God. So I'm going to go through different kinds of words in how they're meant, how they're used, and explain just how significant these words truly are, and why we should all be careful in how we use them, or how we view them.

God's Words:

God says that those who hear His Words and puts them into practice is like a man who "built his house on rock." (Matthew 7:24 NIV). We should admire His Words because they "have supported those who stumbled", and have "strengthened faltering knees" (Job 4:4 NIV). His Words are flawless (Psalm 12:6 NIV), and sweeter than honey (Psalm 119:103 NIV). They are full of Spirit and life (John 6:63 NIV) and if we remain in God and His Words remain in us, we may "ask whatever you wish, and it will be done for you." (John 15:7 NIV) (just remember that it has to be in line with God's will, while also being pure, unselfish, and that when God answers you, it will be in *His* time...the perfect time).

We are to encourage one another with His Words (1 Thessalonians 4:18 NIV), and we should always speak with words of the Spirit, rather than words of human wisdom (1 Corinthians 2:13 NIV). In fact, "If anyone speaks, they should do so as one who speaks the very words of God." (1 Peter 4:11 NIV). That's not to say that you should pretend you're God, because there is only one God. And that's not to say that you're not allowed to have a normal day-to-day conversation. But we should speak the way God has called us to. They (God's Words) are not just idle words, but are our life (Deuteronomy 32:47 NIV), and we should not depart from them, but treasure them more than our daily bread (Job 23:12 NIV).

God says to "Take hold of my Words with all your heart; keep my commands and you will live. Get wisdom, get understanding; do not forget my Words or turn away from them." (Proverbs 4:4-5 NIV), and one good reason may be "For I will give you words of wisdom that none of your adversaries will be able to resist or contradict." (Luke 21:15 NIV). Another good reason may be that "because of His Words many more became believers." (John 4:41 NIV). And once one has God's Word, which is also His Spirit, which is part of who He is, He will "never leave you nor forsake you" (Hebrews 13:5-6 NIV), and that the "words that I have put on your mouth will always be on your lips, on the lips of your children and on the lips of their descendants" (Isaiah 59:21 NIV). So if you're a parent or thinking of becoming one, know that it's also good to have God's Words for those two reasons alone. Another is that His Words carry authority (Luke 4:32 NIV), authority and power to drive out evil spirits (Luke 4:36 NIV); and when I say spirits, think of how there's the spirit of anger, the spirit of hatred, the spirit of jealousy, etc.

So whatever the case, there are many good reasons to grab and keep hold of God's Words, many more than any one man (let alone, all of mankind) could even list, but now let's move on to God's Words through His prophets and His people…

Words of His Prophets and His People:

God has used His prophets to instruct His people (Deuteronomy 18:18 NIV), and for the cause of His people and each of their daily needs (1 Kings 8:59 NIV). The words of His prophets have given wisdom and insight, and the words of God's people are carried out in the same way (that is, if they truly are God's people and not disciples of false prophets). The righteous words spread "to the ends of the world" (Psalm 19:4 NIV), and those who seek them will gain "wisdom and instruction; for understanding words of insight;" (Proverbs 1:2 NIV). In fact, "The wise in heart are called discerning, and gracious words promote instruction." (Proverbs 16:21 NIV). God says to "Apply your heart to instruction and your ears to words of knowledge." (Proverbs 23:12 NIV) and that "The quiet words of the wise are more to be heeded than the shouts of a ruler of fools." (Ecclesiastes 9:17 NIV). He (God) even goes as far as to say (through His Prophet): "Do not speak to fools, for they will scorn your prudent words." (Proverbs 23:9 NIV), and that "Sin is not ended by multiplying words, but the prudent hold their tongues." (Proverbs 10:19 NIV).

"The Lord detests the thoughts of the wicked, but gracious words are pure in his sight." (Proverbs 15:26 NIV), and "Gracious words are a honeycomb, sweet to the soul and healing to the bones." (Proverbs 16:24 NIV). Our words, as God's people, are to come from an upright heart, and to be sincere with what we know (Job 34:4 NIV), and we are to use "words with restraint", and know that "whoever has understanding is even-tempered." (Proverbs 17:27 NIV). But most importantly, we are to "not add to His Words, or he will rebuke you and prove you a liar." (Proverbs 30:6 NIV). So let's move on to the words that are twisted, the words of the liars…the words of the wicked.

The Words of the Wicked:

First of all, let's start with bribes, for all words of the wicked are bribes to try to win us over to the side of the enemy. God says to "not accept a bribe, for a bribe blinds those who see and twists the words of the innocent." (Exodus 23:8 NIV). Now let's move on to just what the words of the wicked do. "All day long they twist my words; all their schemes are for my ruin." (Psalm 56:5 NIV) and "His talk is smooth as butter, yet war is in his heart;" (Psalm 55:21 NIV). I know from God that "The words of the reckless pierce like swords, but the tongue of the wise bring healing." (Proverbs 12:18 NIV), so I know that their words may hurt, but there ARE wise followers of Christ who will always be there to help me, and I know that to the wicked "you have been trapped by what you said, ensnared by the words of your mouth." (Proverbs 6:2 NIV). And as a comfort, God has also said "Do not be afraid of what they say or be terrified by them, though they are a rebellious people." (Ezekiel 2:6 NIV), for "The words of the wicked lie in wait for blood, but the speech of the upright rescues them." (Proverbs 12:6 NIV). So even though the wicked will lie in wait to harm me, I know that in standing up right, in righteousness as a God-fearing Christian, I will be safe, for the Holy Spirit is my advocate (John 14:16, 26-27 NIV). And God will also frustrate the words of the unfaithful (Proverbs 22:12 NIV), even though their gossiping words "are like choice morsels; they go down to the inmost parts." (Proverbs 26:22 NIV), I know that "The Lord is my helper; I will not be afraid. What can mere mortals do to me?" (Hebrews 13:6 NIV). I know that the wicked, "they are conceited and understand nothing. They have unhealthy interest in controversies and quarrels about words that result in envy, strife, malicious talk, evil suspicions" (1 Timothy 6:4 NIV), so why should I even bother listening to them? Especially when God says to "Let no one deceive you with empty words, for because of such things God's wrath comes on those who are disobedient." (Ephesians 5:6 NIV).

So now that we've covered the words of the wicked, remember to remind God's people of these things (2 Timothy 2:14 NIV), but let's move on to our words, and how we should speak when speaking to God (praying).

How We Should Speak to God:

First of all, "Do not be quick with your mouth, do not be hasty in your heart to utter anything before God. God is in heaven and you are on earth, so let your words be few." (Ecclesiastes 5:2 NIV). "And when you pray, do not keep babbling like pagans, for they think they will be heard because of their many words." (Matthew 6:7 NIV). And most importantly, "Humble yourselves before the Lord, and he will lift you up." Other than that, know that God loves you, and he has said: "Ask and it will be given to you; seek and you will find; knock and the door will be opened to you." (Luke 11:9 NIV), so don't be ashamed to ask God for something, because He is the one who is the most loving, most understanding, and most sincere in all existence, and if you pray to Him with an honest and humble heart, and if what you ask is right with his Word, then I'm confident He WILL answer you. Don't expect a "fast-food God", He will respond in His own way, in His timing, and when He does, it'll have been well worth the wait. But have patience, and trust Him, for He loves you above all creatures, and though He may be mysterious, He is the most reliable and a petition to the Lord is far more effective than a petition to man (that's not to say that you can't ask a fellow person for help...we're supposed to help each other).

But now that we have covered how to speak to God, let's move on to just how we should handle His words...

How We Should Handle *His* Words:

First of all, we need to understand that even though God promises us many things, we must keep ourselves in alignment with His Word, His will, His laws, and His decrees. Deuteronomy 29:29 states: "The secret things belong to the Lord our God, but the revealed belong to us and to our children forever, that we may follow all the words of this law." (NIV), and Deuteronomy 29:19 states that "When such a person hears the words of this oath and they invoke a blessing on themselves, thinking "I will be safe, even though I persist in going my own way," they will bring disaster on the watered land as well as the dry."" (NIV). We are to "discern for ourselves what is right" and "let us learn together what is good." (Job 34:4 NIV). We should also always keep in mind that "everyone who hears these words of mine and does not put them into practice is like a foolish man who built his house on sand." (Matthew 7:26 NIV). We should not be ashamed of God's Words, for "the Son of Man will be ashamed of them when he comes in His glory and in the glory of the Father and of the holy angels." (Luke 9:26 NIV). And we should not ignore God's Words, but instead read it all the days of our lives, so that we may learn to "revere the Lord...and follow carefully all the words of this law and these decrees." (Deuteronomy 17:19 NIV).

Remember that when Jesus became incarnate (made into flesh; with us), he established a new covenant, overturning such things as stoning one to death and the like, however, he did leave simple things such as having no other God before him, and a large portion of the nearly 613 or so commandments of the Old Testament in practice. The most important thing we can do in knowing how to handle God's Words is simply to read the Gospels (Matthew, Mark, Luke and John), Acts and Romans, and then once we have a basic understanding of these, carry on through the rest of the New Testament. For those new to the faith, try not to get tangled up in the Book of Revelation...a lot of what's written in it is open to a vast amount of differing interpretations, but first study fervently the books of the Bible prior to it so that you may establish a solid foundation of faith in our Lord and Savior Jesus Christ before moving on to trying to understand such a complex book. When you read Jesus' parables, know that they are examples he is using to demonstrate simple truths, and when he says something in literal terms, don't try to twist it if it makes you uncomfortable...instead, ask God in prayer for the will power, strength and renewing of your mind so that you may come to be accepting of living a more Christ-like lifestyle.

Closing Thoughts on Words:

I didn't offer a dictionary...I didn't offer a thesaurus. Anyone can find those in a bookstore or online. What I did offer is a simple glimpse into how words are used in the Bible, how words are used in life, and how we should use words, according to God's Word. With so many definitions for each and every word, and so many words that no one can even count how many exist in just the English language alone, I hope this helped lay a simple foundation so that when you think of words, before you speak them, and when you hear them, you'll know better what to do with them. But always remember: "For the mouth speaks what the heart is full of." (Luke 6:45 NIV).

Part IV
Lines

"There are no lines in nature, only areas of colour,
one against another."

-Edouard Manet

Do you believe in lines? Do you think that a single line exists anywhere in the universe? Think of one and I'll prove you wrong. Take Lasers for example, highly focused beams of lights, yet they still rely on beams of light, which if you know anything about light, it travels in light waves, like waves of the ocean. Lines drawn by rulers are still going to be bumpy, either because microscopically the ruler has bumps on its edge, or the surface you draw on is microscopically bumpy. Even lines drawn on the microscopic scale would be bubbly, because the smallest elemental particles (which they would be made of) would not be linear in shape. Try to think of any kind of line that you can, and dig deep down to the closest you can possibly imagine or see it, and you'll soon realize that lines are merely a figment of human imagination to make things simple for our brains to process. It's the connecting of dots that allows our minds to draw connections and keep things simple, and for this reason, I like the idea of lines, because sometimes it seems as thought there's not enough time to think more in depth; but when it comes down to it: we need to focus on the figurative lines of speech to better understand just why what we say can never be perfect.

If no lines exist in the universe, then how can what we say ever be perfect? Straight talk, as is called, really is one or more persons trying to get to their points across, but the "lines" still have to be curved or "bent" to the other's needs in order for their points to come across. We try to connect the dots as simply as possible, and it's been said that the shortest distance from one point to another is a straight line, but in knowing that no true lines exist, then how can we do this? We can't.

The point I'm trying to get across is that if we, as humans are innately incapable of saying something perfectly, then how can we expect the words of others to come across in perfection? There is only one entity in all of existence whose words are perfect, and He (God) is in the heavenly realm, and is not creation, but the Creator. Only He can say things perfectly, and only He can move from point A to point B in a straight line, because He's God and He can bend the laws of physics since He established and controls them. He is the only one who can do anything perfect, so please, don't expect any single human being, let alone a group of them, to ever say or do something in perfection.

Part V

Forbearance

"The real or supposed rights of man are of two kinds, active and passive; the right in certain cases to do as we list; and the right we possess to the forbearance of assistance of other men."

-William Godwin

In this section I will break down the meanings of forbearance, and how we should use them in our ways of being, as Christians, as easily as I possible can. There are seven main points I will try to get across, and they are: Patience, Self-Control, Resistance, Tolerance, Moderation, Leniency, and Mercy. So let's start:

Patience:

It's been said that patience is a virtue, but did you know that God requires it of us? (James 5:7-8; Psalm 37:7-9; 1 Thessalonians 5:14). To be patient is to be wise, because if we were to rush things, we could very well miss out on something better God has in store for us. And in being patient with fellow men, it might just be that little bit of extra time that it takes for them to come around and see things the way we do, or vise-versa... them being patient while we take time to mentally sort things out in our minds. Patience in waiting for something to get done, can result in quality over quantity, and patience in a project can give it more time to be better thought out and more well rounded; whereas not having patience could very well end up resulting in a less professional outcome. However you use patience, keep it as a tool for everything in your life. Whether dealing with a spouse, friend, loved one, co-worker, repairman, etc., test your patience and the more of it you gain, the more rewarding you'll find it to be.

Self-Control:

We are to be self-controlled and even-tempered. Else, we act like fools. The Bible calls for us to be of sober mind, awake and alert, always ready and prepared for whatever life might throw at us. If we have not control, then we have only haphazard souls, which we all know will do no good, but produce much distress in this world, for ourselves and to others. So please try and remain in control of yourself, as each and every one of us should, and practice strengthening your self-control, as each time your life will tempt you to. And remember: "For the Spirit God gave us does not make us timid, but gives us power, love and self-discipline." (2 Timothy 1:7 NIV).

Resistance:

We are to resist the enemy, evil, sin, deceit/lies, treacherous schemes, foul play, and anything that God would not approve of. Our prime example is written in the New Testament. Though none of us can ever be as great as Jesus, we can use his life on this earth as an example. Think of all the times he had to resist the enemy from birth to the passion, from the cross to the resurrection. Don't expect yourself to be fully capable of resisting any and every vile thing in this world, for we are all just human, but try your hardest, give it your all, and the more your resist, the easier it will become with God's help!

Tolerance:

We live in a world as diverse as the birds of the sky. There are many different people, with many different faiths. There are many different belief systems and many different ways of being. God's Word tells us "If it is possible, as far as it depends on you, live at peace with everyone." (Romans 12:18 NIV). I know we may not like the way some people are, but how are we to ever win them over to our side if we keep ostracizing them, casting them out from the chance to hear God's Word? Should we not open the doors to them to at least have the chance to feel the presence of God in the company of true believers? I know God says in the last days (of the wicked) to "have nothing to do with such people." (2 Timothy 3:1-5 NIV) and it also says to "Have nothing to do with the fruitless deeds of darkness, but rather expose them." (Ephesians 5:11 NIV). But always keep in mind, when someone is living in sin, "Brothers and sisters, if someone is caught in a sin, you who live by the Spirit should restore that person gently. But watch yourselves or you also may be tempted." (Galatians 6:1 NIV), and, "Jesus answered them, "It is not the healthy who need a doctor, but the sick. I have not come to call the righteous, but sinners to repentance.""(Luke 5:31-32 NIV). We are called to spread God's Word, and to do so gently. If anyone doesn't want to hear it, then that's his or her choice. God gave us free will; the ability to either accept or deny Him. But know that we are called to "fish for people" (Matthew 4:19 NIV), and it's my firm belief that we should try to win over as many people as we can to serve in God's kingdom, because the more of us there are, the more God's Word will spread; and the more God's Word spreads, the better this world becomes.

Moderation:

All things should be taken in moderation. Excess is an indulgence we should share with others who are less fortunate. We only need what our lives require. And to take some things in excess, oh how that kills our quality of life.

Leniency and Mercy:

The Bible says that: "Whoever spares the rod hates their children, but the one who loves their children is careful to discipline them." (Proverbs 13:24 NIV)…this is not the point I'm trying to get at. I believe that some punishments are required to not only prevent spoiled brats from emerging, but that they also help correct people from the errors of their ways. Yet when someone is truly sorry, has stopped what they were doing, and is asking for forgiveness, we, as Christians, should do as Our Father does for us, and forgive. That's all.

Part VI

Forgiveness

"Always forgive your enemies — nothing annoys them so much."

-Oscar Wilde

Some say to "forgive and to forget", well sometimes I find it hard to forget, let alone forgive...but I know that if I do not forgive, then I cannot be forgiven (Matthew 6:15). When someone does something so heinous how can we forgive him or her? There are parts of us, who we are as humans that inherently want to hold grudges and never let go. But the truth is: God endures the worst pains of any soul and still is eagerly waiting to forgive, so long as the sinner asks Him for forgiveness.

That's all it takes for God to forgive, a simple plea...so why can't we be the same way to those who do wrong to us? I think it's nearly impossible to forgive someone if they're still doing what is wronging us, but still...unless we forgive, we cannot be forgiven. It's such a hard task to do, but forgiveness is a muscle that must be exercised as a true Christian, and as difficult as it might be, in the least think of this: to forgive someone is to rid them of any pride they had in doing what they did. It shows them that they can't hurt you, because you're stronger than them. And in doing this, who knows, maybe they'll actually have a change in their way of being and come around to living a life that God would approve of. "But I tell you, love your enemies and pray for those who persecute you," (Matthew 5:44 NIV). Sometimes we can only forgive others with God's help, and to get God's help, it requires we truly are worshippers of Him so that we don't get stuck in a state of bitterness...so let's move onto the next section: Praise, Worship and Thanksgiving.

Part VII

Praise, Worship and Thanksgiving

"Now, our God, we give you thanks, and praise your glorious name."

-1 Chronicles 29:13 NIV

We all know that God loves it when we give Him praise, worship and thanksgiving, but what most of us fail to realize is just how significant this can be in fighting life's battles.

It's a privilege to approach God, bow down before Him and laud Him with our praises and feel His presence within us. The act of raising our eyes and hands to Him, and mouthing our words of praise is an essential part to our Christian... to our spiritual life. God is looking for people to praise Him, and as Jesus said, "Yet a time is coming and has now come when true worshipers will worship the Father in the Spirit and in truth, for they are the kind of worshipers the Father seeks. God is spirit, and his worshipers must worship in the Spirit and in truth." (John 4:23-24 NIV).

When we praise the Lord, our lives are changed in several ways:

- **We Become Connected to Him:**
  "Yet you are enthroned as the Holy One; you are the one Israel Praises." (Psalm 22:3 NIV).
  We are NOT alone! We are in the Holy presence of God, our King, who loves us and is for us!

- **Our Fears are Allayed:**
  "In God, whose word I praise, in the Lord, whose word I praise-in God I trust and am not afraid. What can man do to me?" (Psalm 56:10-11 NIV)
  Our eyes are upon Him and not the circumstance!

- **It Changes Our Outlook:**
  "Praise the Lord. Praise the Lord from the heavens; praise him in the heights above." "Let them praise the name of the Lord, for at his command they were created," (Psalm 148:1, 5 NIV).

- **It Vanquishes the Enemy:**
  "Our God, will you not judge them? For we have no power to face this vast army that is attacking us. We do not know what to do, but our eyes are on you." (2 Chronicles 20:12 NIV).
  "You believe that there is one God. Good! Even the demons believe that—and shudder." (James 2:19 NIV).
  The battle belongs to the Lord. He WILL fight for us. We simply need to remain faithful and obedient to Him, and then we need not fear!

- **Our Love for the Lord is Deepened:**
  "Not to us, Lord, not to us but to your name be the glory, because of your love and faithfulness." (Psalm 115:1 NIV).

  How can our love not grow stronger when the creator of the Universe unconditionally loves us? And to think: He loves when we praise Him, so wouldn't that increase our love of Him? Wouldn't it grow deeper into our hearts, minds and souls?

We can also worship and praise not only through singing and in prayer, but also throughout our lives in all that we do, counting our blessings and thanking God for them each and every day. What an amazing gift that to praise the one who created us all, we receive delight in his sight!

Part VIII
Endurance

"Then Jesus told his disciples, 'If anyone would come after me, let him deny himself and take up his cross and follow me. For whoever would save his life will lose it, but whoever loses his life for my sake will find it. For what will it profit a man if he gains the whole world and forfeits his soul? Or what shall a man give in return for his soul?"

-Matthew 16:24-26 NIV

If we are to follow the examples laid out by Christ then we must first understand what he had to endure during his life incarnate. The following section is merely a glimpse into what he had to endure, so that we may come to realize that what we must endure, is nothing anywhere near what he has.

Anyone who has read the Gospel of Matthew knows a little bit about Christ, but what would be the strongest of themes he held? In order to understand just what Christ went through, the Book of Matthew must be read from beginning to end, with a focus on Christ's endurance. Christ endured hunger, the offer of world domination, spiritual testing, ridicule, back-stabbing, and ultimately, his crucifixion.

Though Christ had an awkward birth (Matthew 1:25) by being born in a less than hospitable environment, as well as a moment of refuge from Herod (Matthew 2:13-18), it is his temptation which truly began him having to endure a great deal of hardships. For starters, he began a spiritual testing of a forty-day journey through a desert, all while fasting. The tempter (Satan) came to him and tried to get him to use his authority to make bread. The tempter then tempted Jesus to use his powers over nature and have angels catch him from a falling. Lastly, the tempter offered Christ dominion over all the land if Christ had simply bowed down to Satan once. Of course, Christ endured all of these and never gave in. But this was just the start to a highly painful ministry which eventually led to him being crucified.

During Christ's ministry, he spoke in parables, metaphors, and symbols to help his audience and enemies understand the true meaning of the "law". This went against the oral traditions of the Pharisaical leadership. This of course, as flipping a laws understanding on its head, would have upset a very many of people.

There are many instances where Christ was ridiculed, mocked, scoffed at, and straight up declared as an enemy of righteousness. The Pharisees considered him to be a heretic; the crowds were mixed with opinions about who he truly is. Imagine walking down a street with a few followers, while the rest of everyone else you encounter sees you as the scum of the earth. Christ went through all this, yet endured.

Christ followed His Words by living them out. He spoke of "not seven times, but seventy-seven times." (Matthew 18:22 NIV) that one should forgive his brother. He said "If anyone slaps you on the right cheek, turn to them the other cheek also." (Matthew 5:39 NIV). Though these sayings can and are interpreted in many ways, nothing stands out louder in them than the overall theme of endurance. After all, Christ endured suffering to the end (but I'll get to that later).

Christ not only lives out a life of endurance, but also calls on his followers to do the same. He says to "take up their cross" (Matthew 16:24 NIV), and to basically leave the flesh to the flesh and go with the spiritual (paraphrased Matthew 8:18-22). To let alone all the physical possessions within a physical world would truly be to endure hardships so strong that reliance on faith must prove wholesome and nourishing. Else, there would be death. But Christ also spoke of just how far to endure. He spoke of enduring till the end.

The higher ranking of Christ's enemies "plotted to arrest Jesus in some sly way and kill him." (Matthew 26:4 NIV). Of course Jesus already knew he had a great deal of enemies, but how could one in the flesh even bear the idea of being put to death? Jesus knew what he was to endure, and no matter how tempting it must have been to scatter and flee, he stood the test and kept on the straight and narrow path. The path which would lead to his crucifixion and the fulfillment of the law.

In order to arrest Jesus, of course those who were to arrest him would have needed to know where to find him. One of

Christ's disciples named Judas Iscariot was just that information bearer. He was the one who ultimately "stabbed Christ in the back". In Matthew 26:15 NIV, it states: "So they counted out for him thirty silver coins." Thirty silver coins was the value that one of Christ's "inner circle" (Judas) valued his life at, and for thirty silver coins, the ultimate of hardships was given way to take place. Christ knew this and in knowing his purpose, he kept on enduring.

Aside from the "normal" day-to-day life of Christ, nothing stands higher than when he went through the elongated torturous, humiliating, and excruciatingly painful crucifixion. He said that it would happen by stating, "As you know, the Passover is two days away—and the Son of Man will be handed over to be crucified." (Matthew 26:2 NIV). Of course Jesus let his closest and twelve original disciples know of what was to happen, even though they could not see why it must take place.

Just before Jesus endured his crucifixion, he had to stand "trial" and amazingly chose to speak only truth, knowing that what was to happen must happen so that the scriptures will be fulfilled (see Matthew 26:54). It's also important to note that Jesus most often didn't even speak back during this "trial", but remained silent, as a silent protester. Unlike any other protester, he had to do this to make sure what was to take place would actually happen so that the sinners could be forgiven.

On the way to his crucifixion, Roman soldiers mocked him, wrapping him in a robe and making up a "crown of thorns" which they jabbed onto the crown of his head. They did this by taking a staff and hitting him repeatedly on the head with it. They also spit on him and mockingly called him, "King of the Jews", yet no matter how severe the Romans made his suffering, Christ endured. (See: Matthew 27:27-31).

Athletes talk of physical endurance, academics talk of mental endurance, but it's hard to find someone willing to endure the worst that life on this planet has to offer...especially when you don't even deserve the least of it. Jesus Christ suffered hunger, temptation to reign over the earth by simply bowing down to Satan, and great spiritual testing. He also endured ridicule, backstabbing, and ultimately, his crucifixion. If one wants to follow in Christ's footsteps, he/she must understand just how much one should endure. The theme of endurance seems to run throughout Christ's life, and in the Gospel of Matthew, is mentioned from beginning to end.

West:

Revelation Field Manual
(Revised, Expanded)

A quick note: Not everything in this book is meant to be taken as literal. Some statements are mere figures of speech, whereas others are straightforward and written to help you prepare yourself for life's battles. Though it might reference the Bible's Book of Revelation, this book is more about learning how to fight the good fight, the way God intended: through peace and perseverance; while preparing you to live each and every day as if the end truly is near, so that you stand prepared for whatever life may throw at you and live each day to the fullest. No matter how big or small the battles your life has in store for you, this book is sure to help you overcome them the Christian way! This book isn't just written for those who are blessed with an overall safe living environment, but is written ESPECIALLY for those who live in areas where having this book would get them killed. Where their faith could get them persecuted, and where the Word of God is merely shunned on or even as far as outlawed. No matter if you are one of those…if you lose this book, lose your Bible, lose any physical Christian item, or have any taken away, never lose your faith and know that even though people may take your life, they can NEVER take your faith and salvation!

Contents:

Part I

What to Expect

NOTE: In times of true crisis, the one's who know the most are the one's who most look to. So be prepared for whatever life may throw at you, and as always: remain adamant in your faith!

Imagine you wake up one day and find a mass casualty event has taken place…only it's not a one-time thing…it's happening every day. Now turn on the news and tell me how that is much different from what already happens day to day in this world. I'm not one to preach that "the end is near", or that it has begun, but I am one to preach that it's better to be prepared, since none of us know when the day or the hour will come; and regardless of whether or not it comes in your lifetime…there's plenty going on as it stands. You might think that with God, all things become easy, but in truth, it's when you choose God that the enemy chooses to strike at you even more. When God offers to let you become a Colonel in His army, the Devil will offer to let you become a General in his. It's this very temptation that makes walking with God seem more difficult…especially if you are currently living in the end times, or in a land where it feels almost as though it is. Though it might not be the end times right now, know that Earth is a finite resource, and eventually, it will end. So it's better to live every day thinking it's the last, so you live every day to its fullest potential. During the end times, things will be more difficult than any other time in history. It is the climax of all creation. After it, comes God's eternal kingdom. To bridge the gap from this life to the next, you have to be prepared for anything the enemy might throw at you. You must constantly stand guard, protecting your heart above all things, because "…everything you do flows from it." (Proverbs 4:23 NIV).

Part II
The Armor of God

The full armor of God consists of:

1: The belt of truth
2: The breastplate of righteousness
3: Feet fitted with readiness of the Gospel
4: The shield of faith
5: The helmet of salvation
6: The sword of the Spirit
(Paraphrased Ephesians 6:13-17 NIV)

THE BELT OF TRUTH is to be fitted around your waste, and is used to carry the Sword of the Spirit. The **BREASTPLATE OF RIGHTEOUSNESS** is to protect your vital organs...your heart. **FEET FITTED WITH READINESS** is being prepared to share the Gospel. The **SHIELD OF FAITH** is made by trusting in God, when the enemy tries to make you doubt Him. Use it to extinguish all the enemy's fiery darts. Remain adamant in your faith! The **HELMET OF SALVATION** is provided free-of-charge, via Jesus Christ. The **SWORD OF THE SPIRIT** is the Word of God. Use it liberally to attack the enemy. Fire at will!

If you're missing any of the six pieces of God's full armor, then that means you have a weak-point with which the enemy will use against you. Also, your armor, as with any armor, must be maintained and taken care of properly. So polish it up regularly, being as Christ-like as possible. You can't give anyone else your armor; however, help them build up their own. Carry the weight of your brother in arms, and leave no man behind. The Bible says, "Though one may be overpowered, two can defend themselves. A cord of three strands is not quickly broken." (Ecclesiastes 4:12 NIV) so use the buddy system, for man is not meant to be alone. With one buddy backing you up, you can both keep watch front-to-back so that the enemy cannot surprise either of you. And when one of you falls, the other will be able to help him up. But it is for this reason that the buddy system should have at least three people. This way, when one falls, and another helps him up, a third can keep watch so that the enemy may not surprise any of you.

Temptation to take off your armor will happen frequently. Every time the enemy strikes at you, though your armor will protect you, you will have an itch urging you to remove it and check for any wounds. Know that if you have on God's armor in full, no attack of the devil will do *ANY* damage! The devil will try to trick you and make you think you're wounded, weak, or unable to carry on so that he can convince you to remove your armor and give up. Don't! You must *never let the enemy's tricks fool you!* If you were to remove your breastplate of righteousness, for example, the enemy can strike at your heart. If you remove your belt of truth, he can attack your loins. If you remove your Sword of the Spirit, that would mean you are in a defenseless fight. God doesn't want you to lose your battles so never give up! Also, make sure that your armor is always tightly fitted and the right size for who you are. Some people have bigger ministries, and need stronger armor, whereas other are simple folk, and only need light armor. However, all armor of God is full and completely capable of defeating any and all of the enemy's attacks when it's put on as a whole.

Part III

The Sword of the Spirit

The Sword of the Spirit is our spiritual weapon of choice. It is the Word of God. It is what we are to use to strike at the enemy, but in any good battle, you must first have a good foothold. In spiritual warfare the enemy will strike in any and every direction, whereas we must aim directly at him. Think of yourself as flying high above the enemy, preparing to bomb him in an air strike. He will fire all his AAA (Anti-Aircraft Artillery) at you in every direction, but our strikes must be pinpoint on his exact location. We must always make sure that it is the *enemy* we are striking down, and not one of our fellow comrades (as in: never attack the sinner...attack the sin). And the root of all sin is the Devil. Don't attack the effect of the sin; attack what causes it. In this long campaign of war with the enemy, we must constantly be on the offensive...striking everywhere he is. But be sure to not cause any collateral damage, harming innocent bystanders (example: judging others instead of helping them grow spiritually). We, as Christians, already have a bad enough "rap" in this world. The enemy has staged his own unrelenting campaign of psychological warfare, trying to brainwash the world against us. We must combat the enemy's propaganda. Anywhere we spot it, as sly and stealthy as it may be, we must confront it and shed truth over the enemy's lies. Remember, all lies are of the enemy, as the Devil is the "father of lies" (John 8:44 NIV).

Our swords must be constantly sharpened, avoiding any dull spots. We must study God's Word continually throughout life, ensuring that we have a thorough knowledge of it. Enough of a thorough knowledge that we could answer any questions with precise, pinpoint accuracy! We also must continually strengthen our arms to be able to carry our swords of the Spirit (as in: we must be strong in faith). We must be able to hold our sword with one hand, and carry a fellow comrade in the other (meaning: being your "brother's keeper"). Our Bibles are our swords and we cannot let them fall into enemy hands. The enemy will twist the words, remove pages and ultimately: try to use our swords against us. We cannot let this happen in *any circumstance!* (Note: That doesn't mean you can't hand out extra Bibles to those who truly need them…just never give YOUR Bible up. And the best way to never lose or give your Bible up is to memorize as much of it as you can.)

It is also good to know the difference from the enemy and someone who just simply doesn't know God's Word. If someone doesn't have a basic understanding of who God truly is, then it is your responsibility to show him or her by living a life God approves of. Teach them by witnessing. Try to win them over with patience and gentleness. Once they get a basic knowledge of whom God is, then help them learn how to sharpen their sword. Teach them how to study God's Word; teach them how to fight with God's Word. Teach them how using God's Word in battle is the most effective of weapons against the enemy.

Our army is small compared to the enemy's, yet our God is bigger than all his army. The devil can never defeat God, but we still constantly need new recruits. This is why you must be on the lookout for any prospective future enlistees in the Christian army at all times. If you spot someone preaching evil, don't consider him or her as a good recruit. Instead, shoot down what they say by speaking God's Word, and then if they are humbled, invite them into living as a Christian.

Someone who is sitting alone, for example, is probably the easiest of people to recruit. All you have to do is simply walk up to them, spark up a conversation and then slowly try to wing the conversation over to that of a Godly one. Get them to question their beliefs in worldly-origins to the point that they start to see that God is real and that he is the point of life. Do everything in your power, without being too pushy, to get the new recruits to learn how to follow Jesus. However, always remain observant so that you don't fall for any of the enemy's traps.

Also, know that you have no authority to "convert" someone… that's between them and God. You are merely here to shed God's light in this cold, dark world.

The devil is sly and has planted landmines all across the globe in pockets of evil where he tries to lure in Christians that they might lose their faith. This is why we must never let down our guard…keeping our spiritual swords on the ready at all times.

To use our swords does take one subject I haven't much discussed yet…faith. We must have adequate faith to know the true power of our weapons. We must keep in faith that our swords, being the Word of God, are from the master of the universe…the creator of all creation, the power that drives life. We must maintain strong enough faith to fight the battles life will throw at us, and must always openly accept any time that God is trying to have us grow our faith. But remember: every time God places you in a position to grow your faith (especially when *you* ask Him to), the devil will throw everything he can at you. So be prepared in knowing this. Also, remember: that "If you have faith as small as a mustard seed, you can say to this mountain, 'Move from here to there' and it will move. Nothing will be impossible for you." (Matthew 17:20 NIV).

351

Part IV
First Aid

It's common knowledge that if someone has a severe wound and is losing a lot of blood, you should apply direct pressure to keep them from bleeding out. In the same sense, whenever the enemy attacks, the right kind of pressure is needed to keep a person from losing his life spiritually. That pressure can be a little bit of simple motivation or encouragement. Sometimes the devil just gives us a scratch...only saying something to us that barely offends our faith. At other times, the devil will send so many fiery arrows after us that it feels as though he's pierced right through our very hearts. Though God says "Do not be deceived: God cannot be mocked. A man reaps what he sows." (Galatians 6:7 NIV), it still hurts us when the world attacks our faith and us as individuals. After all, our faith is the core thing that really matters in life.

When the devil attacks, no matter how big, or strong, or severe the attack, always bear in mind that Jesus has sent His Holy Spirit to comfort us. After all, we cannot bear the struggles of this life alone, let alone having the very devil, himself attack us. One thing to always keep in mind, though, is that while God is omnipresent and can be everywhere at once, the devil is limited and can only be one place at a time. Though he has many dominions working for him throughout the world, Satan is limited in what he can actually do. In fact, the enemy has to ask God permission to attack us, so also keep in mind that God is loving of us and that "No temptation has overtaken you except what is common to mankind. And God is faithful; he will not let you be tempted beyond what you can bear. But when you are tempted, he will also provide a way out so that you can endure it." (1 Corinthians 10:13 NIV). Every time that the enemy attacks us, no matter how severe, we should *always seek God's help first!* We might receive a simple wound from the devil, or we might obtain such a severe blow from him that we feel there is no hope left, but remember that the devil is the father of lies, and is deceitful and trickier than anyone else in history. He might seem to have only bitten you at times, but remember that he is a serpent and that, as with snakebites, there could always be some venom working its way through your veins. So keep watch of how you're doing, and know when to seek help.

Snakebites must be cured with anti-venom, and as with bites from the serpent, we must instantly pray to God for protection and healing. What might seem like a mere puncture from the fangs of the enemy could be like a little drop of yeast which can work its way through the whole batch.

First aid also depends on having adequate knowledge of how to use your environment to help you. It's called "using what you got". You can't be in the middle of a battlefield and always expect an ambulance to arrive any time you get shot. In fact, medics are a rare breed in any battlefield and in the spiritual sense, only few are strong enough to help heal you. This is why you must learn how to cope with blows from the enemy using the Holy Spirit of God. Think of the Holy Spirit as a nice warm fire you work for when you're stranded in the middle of the Antarctic. It's a rare scarcity to have in an environment like that, but once you have it, you don't want to lose it. God's Spirit is given to us freely, so also don't forget to thank and praise Him for it. God says that once you have the Spirit, He will never leave you. He also says to "Be strong and courageous. Do not be afraid or terrified because of them, for the Lord your God goes with you; he will never leave you nor forsake you." (Deuteronomy 31:6 NIV).

We might, at times, feel as though we are "all alone", but always remember that once you have God, *He has you!* He will *always* be with you even if it feels as though He is gone. Sometimes he lets us go through things just to help us grow stronger. In fact, that's the whole point of life, in that we should constantly be growing our faith and trust in God, that we might come to glorify *His* name!

Part V
Fruits of the Spirit

In this world, the word fruit seems to have taken on a whole new meaning, but that could just be a trick of the enemy to keep us from taking the "fruits of the Spirit" seriously. Paul wrote that: "...the fruit of the Spirit is love, joy, peace, forbearance, kindness, goodness, faithfulness, gentleness and self-control. Against such things there is no law." (Galatians 5:22-23 NIV). So let's break that down:

Love is the very definition of what God is. To have God is to have love. To have love, is to have God.

Joy is what God gives us.

Peace is what *His* Spirit gives us.

Forbearance is a muscle that we must exercise.

Kindness is what we should show to others, as with **goodness**. **Faithfulness** should be applied to how we act towards God. **Gentleness** and **Self-Control** are what we are to have when is comes to waiting on God to act, and how we act day to day.

If we lack any one of these, then we know we need a *spiritual cleansing* so that we might grow to be better for God. We must constantly be working to strengthen our fruits of the Spirit and always accept what God has given us freely. All things of God are good; so don't take them for granted. We need to always realize that God is love and that the more we have of Him, the more fulfilled our lives will be.

It is by showing our fruits of the Spirit that the world will recognize us as Christians. If you're living in the end times, of course being recognized as Christian might seem like a bad thing since the Antichrist will be running the world, but bear in mind that there could very well be someone looking for a Christian to help them, and that if you deny Christ before man, He will deny you before the Father. If someone were seeking a Christian to help them find salvation and understand Jesus, then wouldn't it be selfish of you to hide that fact that you are

Christian? Think of yourself as being a medic in a battlefield ridden with casualties. The world *DEPENDS* on *YOU* to help it! So in knowing this, *don't hide the fact that you have God in your life and that He is your salvation and purpose for being alive!*

But if you have denied Christ, repent and He will forgive you (Note: the only unforgiveable sins are blaspheming the Holy Spirit (Mark 3:29) and taking the mark of the beast (Revelation 14:9-12).

Part VI
The Mark of the Beast

Imagine you wake up one day with soldiers at your door asking you to either take a mark or be executed. Seems like the obvious choice would be to just take this mark and move on with your life. But don't be fooled; God will never ask you to take a number! The enemy, in the end, however, will. He will require that you take his mark (666) on your right hand or forehead. Figuratively, choosing to live out the rest of your life denying Christ is like taking the mark of the beast. But be forewarned: taking the mark of the beast is like getting God's sheep branded for the enemy...once they're branded, they belong to him. God says those who do not take the mark will not be able to buy or sell anything during the end times, but don't let this worry you. What you'll eat, or whether or not you'll survive, God is with you. To be executed for not taking the mark seems like a bad idea to mankind, but what is a small second of tightly gripping your faith and being punished for it when compared with eternity in God's Kingdom? Similarly, in the present times, to face persecution for proclaiming ones faith, yet choosing to denounce it to spare one's earthly life is something that most people would choose. But Jesus said, "...whoever disowns me before others, I will disown before my Father in heaven." (Matthew 10:33 NIV). Jesus says to "Look at the birds of the air; they do not sow or reap or store away in barns, and yet your heavenly Father feeds them. Are you not much more valuable than they? Can any one of you by worrying can add a single hour to your life?" (Matthew 6:26-27 NIV). To guard your heart, you must have on the full armor of God.

The enemy will try to confuse us continually till he sees us give in and turn God down. This is exactly what he wants us to do, and doing this is exactly what his purpose of existence has become. He used to be God's favorite angel, leader of worship and praise, till he became jealous of God, and tried to become God himself. Do not be fooled, Satan still thinks of himself as

God, and believes himself to be higher than God; but he knows the truth and he knows that Jesus Christ has already won the battle when he died on the cross and rose himself back up after three days. So always keep this in mind that the battle is already won.

Though we are still living in our own personal battles, God is eternally victorious. The war is over in God's sight, even though we still live in it. Whether or not you're living in the end times is irrelevant. The fact of the matter is that Jesus Christ died on the cross and in doing so, secured our salvation. So don't let the devil trick you into thinking it's okay to give up. *NEVER GIVE UP ON GOD!*

HE DOESN'T GIVE UP ON YOU!

Part VII
Salvation

When it comes to God's salvation, it's better to have it and not need it, than to need it and not have it. Yet we all need it no matter how pure our hearts, minds and lives might be. Daily, we do things without thinking and even commit sins we're unaware of. Only God has the ability to bring our sins to account for judgment, and since this is the case, I personally prefer to ask forgiveness every day...even if I feel I haven't sinned for that day. The Bible says that "Many will say to me on that day, 'Lord, Lord, did we not prophesy in your name, and in your name drive out demons and perform many miracles?' Then I will tell them plainly, 'I never knew you. Away from me, you evildoers!'" (Matthew 7:22-23 NIV). Try your best to not be an evildoer, but know that we are all sinners. We must all try to better ourselves each and every day. A good way to do this is to know the Ten Commandments. We might know the Ten Commandments, but what we fail to realize is that daily, many of us break at least one of them. Also, once we truly trust and accept Jesus as our savior, we will always be His. We may get out of touch in our relationship with Him, but He will always love us unconditionally. He knows the number of hairs on our heads, but we need to always live the best we can...

Let's go over the Ten Commandments:

1: Do not worship any other Gods
2: Do not make any idols
3: Do not misuse the name of God
4: Keep the Sabbath holy
5: Honor your mother and father
6: Do not commit murder
7: Do not commit adultery
8: Do not commit theft
9: Do not bare false witness
10: Do not covet

The **first commandment** is broken any time any of us worship anything other than God himself. It's quite simple: you can only have one pedestal in front of you to bow down to. Whether or not you choose to have God on that pedestal is your choice... but you can only bow down to one master (Matthew 6:24). The **second commandment**, do not make anything an idol, kind of goes along with the first. If you are to make anything other than God, which you worship or bow down to, you have made an idol; which keeps you from salvation. It's very important to not do this. Also, you can't tie God down to being anything made by man. The **third commandment**, not misusing the name of God is saying to not take his name in vein; to not proclaim anything to be of God when it's not; and to not prophesy saying "God says *this* will happen", when you know it won't. The **fourth commandment**, keeping the Sabbath holy is quite simple. Go to church! I personally prefer more than one church service a week (meaning Bible studies, worship services, etc.) but all God requires of you is to go and honor one day out of the week. Pretty simple requirement considering he's constantly focused on us. The **fifth commandment**, honoring your father and mother is another very simple one to understand, but sometimes difficult to follow. We all get frustrated with our parents at times, but remember, your mom held you inside herself for 9 months, and your dad...well, God just says to honor them, so DO IT! The **sixth commandment**, not committing murder seems pretty simple, but realize that slowly killing yourself with an over indulgence of cigarettes, food, or anything else above moderation is poison to your flesh, and murder in God's sight. He says your body is His temple, so honor it and keep it healthy. The **seventh commandment**, not committing adultery seems simple, but remember when Jesus said "But I tell you that anyone who looks at a woman lustfully has already committed adultery with her in his heart." (Matthew 5:28 NIV). The **eighth commandment**, do not steal, can cover every kind of sin. Think about this: if you cheat on your spouse, you've stolen their marriage rights to you; if you murder, you've stolen a life; if you lie, you've stolen the truth. So to not steal, or commit theft, can be a much broader commandment with an open mind. The **ninth commandment**, not baring false witness, or lying, is quite simple. To say anything other than truth, with the intent of misleading someone, is lying. Don't confuse this with concealment, which is not saying anything at all. Lying is a deliberate action and God forbids it! The **tenth commandment**, not to covet, seems easy to follow, but there's a reason it's the last one of the Ten. You can go through all the commandments and successfully follow them, but then realize your neighbor has a better life, or watch TV and start coveting over something on a commercial, something you don't have...and God doesn't want us to do this. He expects us to be thankful for what He has given us already. We don't need to act like spoiled little brats. After all, what God has given us is *from God!* Who else can give so perfectly and with such good timing? We might lose patience with His timing, but in the end, we always know He's right.

Part VIII
Perseverance

It's when we're almost at the end that the devil tries to trick us to make us give up. It's like running a race and nearing the finish line. The ones you are competing with will do everything to make you give up so that they win. We must constantly keep focus on what is at stake. We need to always stay in line with God's will and never lose sight of the pearly gates. Think of them as the light at the end of the tunnel. The only reason it seems dark is because you're in a place where the light is blocked. In order to see the light, you must do everything in your power to push on and keep on fighting the good fight.

The enemy knows that you just read this. He knows that you may feel like giving up right now, or if not now, some other time in the near future; but never lose hope. The battle is already won through our Lord and Savior Jesus Christ so remain steadfast in spirit.

A funny thing to know about perseverance, is that it's only written in the New Testament. The testament of Jesus Christ!

When Jesus was facing what is known as the Passion, he not only had to be crucified. He was beaten, abused, mutilated, humiliated, and barely had enough strength to carry on. Even though He is Lord, it still was a struggle for Him, yet He chose to remain in love with us, and persevere till the end. When He was hanging on the cross He could have just said "Okay guys, I give up...you win. Now let me down from here." But instead He chose to remain utterly adamant, because He knew what was at stake...both literally and figuratively. God's gift for us in salvation is an eternal blessing. After the 70 or so years we get to live in this life, we move on to an eternal bliss so indescribable that all we really know is we'll be so happy we won't be able to help but constantly be praising, thanking, and worshiping God.

In order to remain perseverant, we must keep on our armor, our *FULL armor,* remain in prayer throughout the day, and rely solely on our Lord, God, and His Holy Spirit to sustain us.

It is also good that in prayer, we should ask for God to guide, direct, surround and protect us with legions upon infinite legions of His mighty warrior angels so that we have an even stronger army; and to also ask God to heal us physically, spiritually, mentally and emotionally.

In prayer, I pray that God guides us so we're on the right path, directs us, so that we know how to act, surrounds us, so that we are in good and graceful company, and protects, so that we are wholly safe. I also ask that He heals us physically, so that we might perform the tasks he has planned for us, spiritually, so that we remain in His will, mentally, so that we can think of sound mind, and emotionally, so that we cannot be weakened the way that the devil wants us to. When we are weakened, we feel like giving up. And this is why I include this in prayer...so that we ultimately persevere. But don't just pray...praise too! Another thing to help with perseverance is knowing that it's the blood of Jesus that sets us free. Many people today are sickened by thinking of blood, because atrocities happen, and this makes people associate blood with death, when in actuality, it is blood that comes from the wellspring of life (our hearts) to keep us alive.

In the sense of the second death, the blood of Jesus keeps us from it. It is our promissory note to enter into Heaven. We should also frequent the act of communion. Remembering what it is that Jesus went through just so that we might live in the next life. He gave His life so that we might live, and when one lays down his life, he is laying down all that he has. All the time and money He could have made...all laid down for us. All the experiences in life He could have had; all laid down for us. So when Jesus laid down His life, know that He was giving all of Himself to us and our salvation. He loves us so much that he persevered through the most painful, agonizing, humiliating and mentally abusing forms of death that anyone can...crucifixion. Imagine being put on display for mockers, as you are nailed to a cross. Even if you're in the end times or not, and are threatened with execution for believing in Jesus, know that no matter how painful your death might be, Jesus first experienced it for you. He won't let you go through more than He went through. And think of where He is now...sitting in Heaven eagerly waiting the appointed time to return.

Part IX

Conclusion

End times, or not, it's always absolutely necessary to be right with God. Even if you aren't living in the end times, your salvation is still at stake if you're not right with Him. I'd suggest as Paul says in 1 Thessalonians 5:17 NIV to "pray continually". There are always a lot of people who need prayer, and I firmly believe that it is our responsibility as Christians to pray for those who aren't saved. It is our responsibility to act according to God's will, and if you want to know whether or not you're acting in *His* will, refer to the Bible. The Bible is God's own personal testimony to us to explain how we're supposed to live in this life, and without it, we are aimlessly doomed to crash right into any and all of the enemy's attacks. Study God's Word so much that it becomes embedded in your innermost being. So much so that every thought you have comes attached with thoughts from Bible verses, so that you'll always have God in mind. If you have God in mind, then He is in you. If He is in you, then where else does He have to go except to pour out from you onto others? God is the best driver of all, so I'd suggest letting Him take control of your life at all times, because we all know that when we have control, that's when things tend to get messed up! It's when flesh controls flesh that sin is born. Take all the pain, suffering, and sorrow you've ever felt, multiply it by how many billions of people have ever lived, and know that this is all caused by sin. It is sin that makes God cry. So know that every second you walk out of line with God, you are just adding to the multitudes of sorrow He feels for us. Try to be your best at all times, and always remember the verse that says "If anyone, then, knows the good they ought to do, and doesn't do it, it is sin for them." (James 4:17 NIV). Always know that the more of God you have in your heart, the more pure your heart is. The more pure your heart is, the better it will be at helping others grow stronger in faith. And that is our ultimate goal in life...to grow in faith so that we might come to glorify God and the name of God. Humbling ourselves before the Lord in prayer, understanding that we are nothing without Him, and earnestly seeking Him and to glorify Him. Always remember that Jesus is the only way to salvation and that without Him, there can be no salvation in your life. Be forgiving to others, as God requires it; and lastly, meditate on where you are right now in your spiritual walk with God. See to it that where you are (in terms of being with God) is always one step closer than the last time you checked...and check yourself daily.

Part X
Quick Reference

(Useful terms related to Revelation)

QUICK REFERENCE:

144,000 – Those from the twelve tribes of Israel sealed for God's protection

Abyss - Place of imprisonment for Satan and his demons before the end.

Apocalypse – Means "the unveiling"; also used to describe the Seven years of the Great Tribulation.

Antichrist – See "Satan". Also, anything that is against (anti) Christ.

Babylon – The enemy's end-times kingdom

The Beast – See "Lucifer"

The Crucifixion – When Jesus paid the price for our sins by dying on the cross, and then raised himself back after three days.

Dragon - See "Lucifer".

False Prophet – Satan, The Antichrist, anyone claiming something that goes against God's word.

Great Tribulation – Period of roughly Seven years where Satan reigns as king of the Earth.

Hades – Hell

Hell – Eternal punishment for unrepentant sinners; ex: Those who don't accept Christ; permanent separation from God, and since all things good are of God…permanent separation from anything good.

Holy City – Jerusalem.

Holy Spirit – Our comforter and is the Spirit of God.

Jesus Christ – Lord of Lords, King of Kings, Savior, Messiah, Son of God.

Lake of Fire – Think of it as a second Hell, after the end is fulfilled, those who take the mark of the Beast, those who don't accept Christ, and those who are of the Devil (including Satan himself) are cast here for eternal punishment.

Lucifer – The Devil, Satan, The Enemy, Father of Lies, All Things Bad. Evil. Sin.

Mark of the Beast - "666" in/on right hand or forehead.

Millennium – The thousand-year reign of Christ after the Seven-year end times is fulfilled.

Multitudes in White Robes – Those who accept Christ before the end; so many that they cannot even be counted

New Heaven, New Earth – After Great Tribulation, God creates a new kingdom. One which will last for eternity.

The Passion – See "Crucifixion".

Rapture – When Jesus brings those who accepted Him up to be with him.

Second Death – Eternal death for those who don't accept Christ. Saved Christians are saved from this "second death," as they are allowed into Heaven.

Sin – Any act against God or God's will.

Seven Seals:

1) White horse; it's rider is given a crown and he is bent on conquest.

2) Red horse; it's rider given power to take peace from the Earth and make men kill each other.

3) Black horse; it's rider holding a pair of scales. Things get expensive.

4) Pale horse; it's rider is named Death and Hell follows behind him.

5) White robe given to each martyr.

6) Great earthquake, Sun blackened, moon turns blood red. Stars fall from sky, and the sky rolls up.

7) Silence in Heaven for about 30 minutes, angels given Trumpets.

Seven Trumpets:

1) Hail, Fire, Blood hurled on the Earth. A third of Earth, trees, and grass burned up.

2) Huge Mountain on fire thrown into the sea. One third of ships and sea creatures are destroyed.

3) One third of waters turn bitter from star falling on them

4) A third of the Sun, Moon, and Stars struck so that a third of the night and day is darkened.

5) Star falls and opens up the Abyss. Sun and Sky darkened by smoke. Locusts harm men without God's seal. Lasts 5 months

6) Four Angels from Euphrates River released to kill one-third of mankind.

7) Jesus reigns

Seven Bowls:

1) Ugly and painful sores on those who have taken the mark of the beast.

2) Sea turns to blood; all sea-creatures die.

3) Rivers and Springs of Water turn to blood.

4) Sun scorches people with fire.

5) The Beasts kingdom thrown into darkness.

6) Demons gather kings of the Earth to wage war on God.

7) It is done.

The Seven Years – Satan reigns as king of the Earth for Seven years. He marauds around the globe trying to make people worship him; pretending he's God. Also known as the Great Tribulation.

The Thousand Years – Jesus reins king for a thousand years, then after that God takes over.

Trinity – The triune God. Father, Son (Jesus), and Holy Spirit.

Revelation Timeline:

-There will be a Seven year peace treaty. In the first three and a half years of this, the world will have peace. Shortly after these years, there will be another three and a half years of Great Tribulation.

-The Antichrist is the one who will form and establish this treaty with the governments of the world.

-At the middle of the Seven years, when the greater calamities begin, the Antichrist (ruler of the world) will require everyone to take his mark (666) on/in their right hands or foreheads. Anyone who rejects this mark will not be able to buy or sell; but those who take it will be banned from salvation and not allowed into the eternal kingdom of God.

-That's about all you need to know in this.

Closing Thoughts

Contents:

This Journey Ends...Yours Begins:

Like I said in the beginning, this isn't your typical book. I hope this "journey" has brought you to grow stronger in your faith, and even more open to God, with a greater love for Him. Even though this book was written with YOU in mind, always know that there's a vast amount of books written as a love letter JUST FOR YOU: God's Word, the Holy Bible.

I've included some extra segments following this closing. Some verses to help along your way through your life's journey, some verses to help those who need to build up confidence, a mini-book to help anyone become a disciple, and if you already are one, maybe there'll be something hidden in it to help you become just a little bit more of a disciple. We've all been called by God to help and uplift each other, and to carry each other's cross, so I pray that you've found this book useful, and that you continue in your journey...that amazing and beautiful gift God's given you: the rest of your life!

With Love and Prayer,
-Chris

Some Verses to Help Along Your Way:

God's Plans For You:

"'For I know the plans I have for you,' declares the Lord, 'Plans to prosper you and not to harm you, plans to give you hope and a future.'"

-Jeremiah 29:11 NIV

Who God Works For:

"And we know that in all things God works for the good of those who love him, who have been called according to his purpose."

-Romans 8:28 NIV

How to Receive the Spirit:

"Peter replied, 'Repent and be baptized, every one of you, in the name of Jesus Christ for the forgiveness of your sins. And you will receive the gift of the Holy Spirit.'"

-Acts 2:38 NIV

Simple Truths:

Read ALL of Matthew Chapter 7 (it's short, you can read it one simple section at a time. These are the parables of Jesus, which will significantly help you along your way.

How to Avoid Falling:

"...If you do not stand firm in your faith, you will not stand at all."

-Isaiah 7:9 NIV

Carrying Each Other's Cross:

"Again, when a righteous person turns from their righteousness and does evil, and I put a stumbling block before them, they will die. Since you did not warn them, they will die for their sin. The righteous things that person did will not be remembered, and I will hold you accountable for their blood."

-Ezekiel 3:20 NIV

Winning Good Favor; Finding the Right Path:

"Let love and faithfulness never leave you; bind them around your neck, write them on the tablet of your heart. Then you will win favor and a good name in the sight of God and man. Trust in the Lord with all your heart and lean not on your own understanding; in all your ways submit to Him, and He will make your paths straight."

-Proverbs 3:3-6 NIV

Being Lifted Up:

"The Lord upholds all who fall and lifts up all who are bowed down."

-Psalm 145:14 NIV

Being a Young Example:

"Don't let anyone look down on you because you are young, but set an example for the believers in speech, in conduct, in love, in faith and in purity."

-1 Timothy 4:12 NIV

Grow in Confidence:

"So we say with confidence, "The Lord is my helper; I will not be afraid. What can mere mortals do to me?""

-Hebrews 13:6 NIV

Loving Wisdom:

"Do not forsake wisdom, and she will protect you; love her, and she will watch over you."

-Proverbs 4:6 NIV

The Armor of God:

"Finally, be strong in the Lord and in his mighty power. Put on the full armor of God, so that you can take your stand against the devil's schemes. For our struggle is not against flesh and blood, but against the rulers, against the authorities, against the powers of this dark world and against the spiritual forces of evil in the heavenly realms. Therefore put on the full armor of God, so that when the day of evil comes, you may be able to stand your ground, and after you have done everything, to stand. Stand firm then, with the belt of truth buckled around your waist, with the breastplate of righteousness in place, and with your feet fitted with the readiness that comes from the gospel of peace. In addition to all this, take up the shield of faith, with which you can extinguish all the flaming arrows of the evil one. Take the helmet of salvation and the sword of the Spirit, which is the word of God. And pray in the Spirit on all occasions with all kinds of prayers and requests. With this in mind, be alert and always keep on praying for all the Lord's people."

-Ephesians 6:10-18 NIV

Give it to God:

"Cast your cares on the Lord and he will sustain you; he will never let the righteous be shaken."

-Psalm 55:22 NIV

Finding Rest in Discomfort:

"Come to me, all you who are weary and burdened, and I will give you rest."

-Matthew 11:28 NIV

Love Defined:

"Love is patient, love is kind. It does not envy, it does not boast, it is not proud. It does not dishonor others, it is not self-seeking, it is not easily angered, it keeps no record of wrongs. Love does not delight in evil but rejoices with truth. It always protects, always trusts, always hopes, always perseveres."

-1 Corinthians 13:4-7 NIV

Lose your pride:

"You may say to yourself, "My power and the strength of my hands have produced this wealth for me." But remember the Lord your God, for it is He who gives you the ability to produce wealth, and so confirms His covenant, which He swore to your ancestors, as it is today."

-Deuteronomy 8:17-18 NIV

Who to Call:

"Call to me and I will answer you and tell you great and unsearchable things you do not know."

-Jeremiah 33:3 NIV

Who to Obey:

"Peter and the other apostles replied: 'We must obey God rather than human beings.'"

-Acts 5:29 NIV

Seeking Guidance?

"Teach me, Lord, the way of your decrees, that I may follow it to the end. Give me understanding, so that I make keep your law and obey it with all my heart. Direct me in the path of your commands, for there I find delight. Turn my heart toward your statutes and not toward selfish gain. Turn my eyes away from worthless things; preserve my life according to your word. Fulfill your promise to your servant, so that you may be feared. Take away the disgrace I dread, for your laws are good. How I long for your precepts! In your righteousness preserve my life."

-Psalm 119:33-40 NIV

Foolishness Destroys:
"Yet these people slander whatever they do not understand, and the very things they do understand by instinct-as irrational animals do-will destroy them."

-Jude 1:10 NIV

Spiritual Sustenance:
"Create in me a pure heart, O God, and renew a steadfast spirit within me. Do not cast me from your presence or take your Holy Spirit from me. Restore to me the joy of your salvation and grant me a willing spirit, to sustain me."

-Psalm 51:10-12 NIV

The Wife of Noble Character:
Read all of Proverbs 31:10-31

Is it sin or not?
"If anyone, then, knows the good they ought to do and doesn't do it, it is sin for them."

-James 4:17 NIV

Why We Need God:
"for all have sinned and fall short of the glory of God,"

-Romans 3:23 NIV

Do this for God:
"I seek you with all my heart; do not let me stray from your commands. I have hidden your Word in my heart that I might not sin against you."

-Psalm 119:10-11 NIV

A Promise from the Lord:

"The Lord will keep you from all harm-he will watch over your life; the Lord will watch over your coming and going both now and forevermore."

-Psalm 121:7-8 NIV

Bible Verses to Help Build Self-Confidence:

For anyone struggling with confidence, having a lack of it, either spiritually or in life in general, I highly encourage you to take this journey: devote an entire day (or however long you see fit) to finding these scriptures and studying them fervently…maybe even scribing them down to help them sink in to your long term memory. Take them in to your innermost being, and allow them (these words from God) to become your confidence. Make the Lord your confidence, and His word his promise to you! What the enemy says to try and bring you down will easily be overcome by these verses, because they are words directly from the One who is above all; Our Father!

Philippians 4:13
2 Timothy 1:7
Hebrews 13:6
Psalm 139:13-14
Hebrews 10:35-36
Ephesians 4:29
Proverbs 3:6
Psalm 138:8
Psalm 27:3
Galatians 2:20
1 John 4:18
Philippians 4:4-7
Philippians 1:6
Luke 14:8-11
Joshua 1:9
Psalm 91:1-16
Ephesians 4:32
1 Corinthians 2:3-5
Proverbs 3:1-26
1 Corinthians 13:1-13

2 Corinthians 12:9
1 Timothy 4:12
Matthew 6:34
Hebrews 4:16
James 1:12
2 Peter 1:3
Romans 8:28
Hebrews 11:1-40
1 Peter 3:10
John 3:16
Proverbs 29:25
Luke 6:31
Psalm 23:1-6
Ephesians 2:9
Romans 8:1-39
Psalm 27:1-2
1 Peter 4:8
Philippians 2:14
Psalm 42:5
Acts 1:8
John 13:34-35
Jeremiah 17:7-8
Deuteronomy 32:10
2 Timothy 1:12
Romans 8:32
Romans 12:3
Psalm 46:1-11
1 Peter 3:9
Romans 8:30
John 15:26
Matthew 18:10
Isaiah 1:1-31
2 Chronicles 16:9
Jude 1:1-25

2 Timothy 2:1
Ephesians 1:18-23
Luke 5:13
Habakkuk 3:17-19
Philippians 3:10
Hebrews 1:1
1 Samuel 12:20
Hebrews 13:5
Jeremiah 11:7
Jeremiah 1:6-9
1 Samuel 1:1-28
1 John 5:14-15
1 Samuel 12:1-25
Exodus 3:10-4:14

How to be a Disciple

Contents:

Introduction

We've all heard of the 12 Biblical disciples (apostles) of Jesus. We all know that they were all humans just as we are. What we don't always know is how to be a disciple God would approve of.

In this mini-book I will discuss not only what a disciple is, but also how we, as followers of Christ, can become better disciples for Him.

In Part One, I will discuss the definition of a disciple. What it is to be one, and how being a disciple of Christ is far more demanding than being a disciple of anyone or anything else. In Part Two, I will discuss forgiveness. Not only how it applies to being a disciple, but also how it's required of us to *be* forgiving. In Part Three, I will discuss what I call "spiritual cleansing". The cleansing that is needed for what I describe in the Fourth Part, which is spiritual growth. Pretty simple to know what I'm talking about, but doing it is a whole different thing. In Part Five, I will explain how hope is not only necessary, but required by God to be a good disciple. In Part Six, I will talk about how trust is one of the most important overlooked qualities we need to have for God to be the way He wants us. And finally, in Part Seven, I will talk about the one thing we all lack: patience.

Of course to be a good disciple, it takes a whole lot more than just reading a book, it demands studying God's Word with diligence, helping others where God calls us to, and most importantly: *LIVING OUR LIVES THE WAY HE COMMANDS!*

Part I
Definition of a Disciple

Let's start by reading a verse from John:
"By this everyone will know that you are my disciples,
if you love one another."
- John 13:35 NIV

When Jesus is speaking about how to be recognized as His disciples, it's a no-brainer that He had to include love. By loving one another you are acting in a way which pleases God. But this also makes it a commandment; that to be recognized as a disciple of Christ, you MUST love one another.

But what is a disciple? A disciple is defined as one who studies a discipline. So to be disciples of Christ, we not only have to have love, we also have to study under Christ. Learn his teachings, delve into their meanings, absorb His message, and then try to become as much like Him as possible.

Moses, The Pharisees, John the Baptist...they all had disciples, but the goal of this book is for us to become better disciples of Christ. Everyone who is a disciple of someone other than God is a disciple of one who is not perfect. I don't know about you, but I'd rather be a disciple of someone who *is* perfect so that I know I'm not only learning from a pure source of wisdom, but that I'm also on my way to being purified.

Part II
Getting Forgiveness

Let's start by reading a verse from Luke:

"...Forgive and you will be forgiven."
- Luke 6:37 NIV

It would be a nice life if we didn't have to have forgiveness. Imagine a world where everything is perfect...no one does wrong, and no one has any expenses. But the world isn't that way and because of the sin we humans commit, forgiveness is actually a blessing considering how much we really have made God hurt over the years.

If someone were to hit you, and then ask forgiveness while honestly feeling bad, they might have learned a lesson to not hit you anymore. However, if someone were to hit you continually while still asking forgiveness, how could you forgive him or her if they keep on hitting? In the same sense, we must ask God for forgiveness *only when we are truly sorry and will do our best to not commit that sin again.* But in order to have forgiveness, it is required of us to be forgiving to those who do sin against us. How can we expect God to forgive if we ourselves aren't forgiving?

Part III

Spiritual Cleansing

Let's start by reading a verse from Proverbs:

"Who can say, "I have kept my heart pure; I am clean and without sin?""

- Proverbs 20:9 NIV

Of course we all know the answer to that is JESUS! However, doesn't the Bible say that we are to try our best to become as much like Him as possible? After forgiving others so we can be forgiven, we need to be cleansed of our old ways. Not only to be renewed in our minds (Romans 12:2), but also to have anything which is the appearance of evil, removed (Ephesians 5:3).

It's important for us to take a shower every day, because dirt, among other things, makes ourselves unclean. In the same way, we should daily be cleansed of our sins, asking God with humble and contrite hearts, to forgive us as we are nowhere near perfect. This allows us the freedom to start the day off clean. It also makes it easier for us to catch any "slips" during the day where we fall because of "getting in the flesh".

Think about it this way: if you don't have any sin on when you wake up, then one splash of muddy sin will stand out unlike if you were already covered with it. Plus it makes us have more freedom to worship God in our lives the way that pleases Him, with *"...a broken and contrite heart."* (Psalm 51:17 NIV)

Part IV
Growing

Let's start by reading a verse from 2 Peter:
"But grow in the grace and knowledge of our Lord and Savior Jesus Christ...."
- 2 Peter 3:18 NIV

Funny how knowledge comes after grace. Remember that "...it is by grace you have been saved...." (Ephesians 2:8 NIV). What I'm getting at here is that in order for us to have the kind of spiritual growth we desire, we must first acknowledge the fact that Christ gave us His grace to save us. It's because of Jesus that we even have the ability to be alive this very moment!

Now, onto the tougher part...the knowledge of Christ. How can we grow to have His infinite knowledge? In this life we can't. Our brains would probably explode if any of us even had a fraction of His true knowledge. But we can have what He has allowed, which is knowledge offered divinely through the scriptures, and revelation knowledge (where God reveals to us somewhat like epiphanies).

Part V
Hope

Let's start by reading a verse from Jeremiah:

"For I know the plans I have for you," declares the Lord, "plans to prosper you and not to harm you, plans to give you hope and a future."
-Jeremiah 29:11 NIV

Obviously God IS in love with us! We might not always know where He wants us to go, or what He wants us to do, but we can rest assured knowing that His plans for us always include divine hope. God doesn't want us believing the lies of the enemy, or anything that would keep us from growing on the path He has for us. God wants us to thrive in this life, not just in Heaven. He has plans to prosper us and to not harm us. But in order for us to have this, we must TRUST in Him.

Part VI
Trust

Let's start by reading a verse from 2 Samuel:
"Sovereign Lord, you are God! Your words are trustworthy, and you have promised these good things to your servant."
- 2 Samuel 7:28 NIV

We have to start off first by acknowledging that God is trustworthy. Anything He says comes into existence, which means anything He says has to be true. God can't lie. Then we can move onto learning how to trust Him.

In order to trust God, I believe you have to go through some struggles. That's not to say that someone couldn't be born just naturally trusting Him, I just believe that God allows us to strengthen our trust in Him through trials and tribulations. This is why we go through stuff...to learn *how* to trust Him.

Part VII
Patience

433

Let's start by reading a verse from Colossians:

"Therefore, as God's chosen people, holy and dearly loved, clothe your-selves with compassion, kindness, humility, gentleness and patience."
- Colossians 3:12 NIV

Let's start by acknowledging that we ARE God's chosen people. Secondly, acknowledging that He has made us holy and has loved us dearly. Then, let us conform to the design which He has made us to which is to have "compassion, kindness, humility, gentleness and patience." After this, know that we are alive. Lastly, knowing that if we are in fact alive, it's because He still has plans for us. If He still has plans for us, then isn't it necessary to remain patient, knowing that the Almighty has something in store for each and every one of us? By His Spirit we are alive!

SPECIAL THANKS:

God – For not only creating, saving, and loving me, but simply because you are who and how you are

Carol Downs – For instilling in me a faith at a young age (3)

Stephen Downs – For teaching me how to teach

Andrea Belau – For her honest critiquing and editing of this book

Pam Blanco – For her help in editing this book, and being my aunt

All others who helped me with this book

My family – For all the ups and "Downs" they've given me

Fellow believers – For doing God's work...I look forward to meeting you someday

My acquaintances – For the simplest of things you've said which have inspired me

You – For reading and using this book...I sincerely hope it not only helps not just you, but all those whom you affect

And of course: all those who've supported me along the way, all those who've corrected me in my life, all my mentors, and all those whose names I haven't mentioned...because everyone I know matters.

For those who are curious, as you recall, I began this book with the word "start". I will not close this book with a finish, as it is about the Christian life, and even though a Christian may die in this life, the Christian life has no end.

...CONTINUE

NOTES: _____

_____

_____

_____

_____

_____

_____

_____

_____

_____

_____

_____

_____

_____

_____

\rule{10cm}{0.4pt}

\rule{10cm}{0.4pt}

\rule{10cm}{0.4pt}

\rule{10cm}{0.4pt}

\rule{10cm}{0.4pt}

\rule{10cm}{0.4pt}

\rule{10cm}{0.4pt}

\rule{10cm}{0.4pt}

\rule{10cm}{0.4pt}

\rule{10cm}{0.4pt}

\rule{10cm}{0.4pt}

\rule{10cm}{0.4pt}

\rule{10cm}{0.4pt}

\rule{10cm}{0.4pt}

\rule{10cm}{0.4pt}